Lucy Jones is a writer and journalist especially interested in the psychological relationship between humans and the rest of nature. Her first book, *Foxes Unearthed*, won the Society of Authors' Roger Deakin Award and her second, *Losing Eden*, explored the link between mental health and nature. She spends as much time as possible outside with her children.

Kenneth Greenway is the Cemetery Park Manager of Tower Hamlets Cemetery Park in London. He has worked in nature conservation for almost twenty-five years and has two decades of experience working with children in natural spaces, including running forest schools. He has two children and spends most of his time immersed in the living world.

Ken's eldest, Amelia, holding a female emperor dragonfly at the Soanes Centre, Tower Hamlets Cemetery Park

Lucy Jones &
Kenneth Greenway

The Nature Seed

How to Raise Adventurous and Nurturing Kids

SOUVENIR
PRESS

First published in Great Britain in 2021 by
Souvenir Press,
an imprint of Profile Books Ltd
29 Cloth Fair
London
EC1A 7JQ

www.profilebooks.co.uk

Image credits: Photographs are courtesy of the authors unless specified below. Image on p. 39 © Kevin Maskell/Alamy Stock Photo; p. 41 © Pix/Alamy Stock Photo; p. 42, right © blickwinkel/Alamy Stock Photo; p. 69 © John Richmond/Alamy Stock Photo; p. 118 © Gillian Pullinger/Alamy Stock Photo. The nettle soup recipe on p. 159 is taken from *Wild Food: A Complete Guide for Foragers* by Roger Phillips, © Roger Phillips 1983, reproduced with permission of the Licensor through PLSclear.

Design by James Alexander/www.jadedesign.co.uk

1 3 5 7 9 10 8 6 4 2

Printed and bound in Italy by L.E.G.O. Spa

A CIP catalogue record for this book is available from the British Library.

ISBN 978 1 78816 797 0
eISBN 978 1 78283 850 0

Lucy: For Skylark, Swift, Wren and Jim,
who carries us all.

Kenneth: To my Mum and Dad who allowed me to follow
my heart, and to my wife Zoe who stands by me, and
for the two mighty girls in my life, my daughters, Amelia
and Elsie, you're my most treasured and entertaining
adventure. This book is for you all! Thank you.

Ken's youngest, Elsie, showing off her muddy hands ... dirt-tastic!

Chapter One

A New, Old Playground

If a child is to keep alive his inborn sense of wonder ... he needs the companionship of at least one adult who can share it, rediscovering with him the joy, excitement and mystery of the world we live in.

Rachel Carson, *The Sense of Wonder*, 1965

In the beginning, before there were crayons and balls, building blocks and books, there was nature. The oldest playground in the world is the natural world. It's where our hunter-gatherer ancestors lived, side by side with wildlife, plants, birds, lakes, trees, rain, snow and wind. Of course it wasn't 'nature', it was just ... home. Playing in nature, then, is one of the most ancient activities on Earth. Parents spending time with their children outside has been the human way for millennia. Children exploring the various loose parts of the outdoors, roaming free in open space, finding roosts and making dens to hide in, and learning through outdoor play, risk and discovery has always been a hallmark of early life.

Well, until recently. Today, for the first time in human history, we in the industrialised West spend between 1 and 5 per cent of our time outside. Our children are enclosed in classrooms and houses and cars and, for various powerful and systemic reasons, feeling engaged and connected with the natural world is not a universal experience.

This matters. A relationship with nature should be a birthright for everyone. Contact with the wild gives all of us opportunities for restoration, peace, creativity, awe, joy, rootedness, self-esteem, fun, resilience and wonder.

The Nature Seed is for anyone with a child in their life who wants to foster and nurture their – and their own! – bond with nature. We begin with babies and children in their early years and journey through middle childhood until the age of eleven or so, looking forward to adolescence. The book is filled with ideas, tips and techniques tailored to different age groups, for families living in both the countryside and the city. Your local nature patch might be a town cemetery, the verges on an estate or an urban woodland. It might be a pond or a river or the sea. You might have a garden or a balcony or a windowsill.

This book has suggestions for activities that can be used in various environments, and a philosophy that can be utilised in even the most urban areas. Our ideas and ethos are drawn from Ken's significant expertise gained from decades of extensive experience in environmental education, working with children outdoors and with his own young daughters; and from Lucy's time spent in nature with her children, and her years of working as a journalist and author, writing about science, environment and health for national newspapers and magazines.

Although it might seem that those in rural areas have greater opportunities to commune with the living world, the estrangement from nature applies across the UK. We live in a country where wildlife species are in grave decline, woodlands and green spaces are threatened and access to nature is unequal. Concurrently, habitats for learning through the senses, imaginative play and involvement with the more-than-human world are depleted, too. We can fight against the systems of destruction and inequality and, in the meantime, we can work with what we've got. Even in the most nature-deprived areas, you will find moments of wonder and awe.

The philosophy and loose method of *The Nature Seed* aim to be accessible for all. We do not yet live in a fair and just society. Nature deprivation is driven by a constellation of socioeconomic and cultural factors. Class, income and ethnicity influence a person's relationship to nature. Black, Asian and minority ethnic people may experience hostility and racism in natural spaces, and those living in deprived neighbourhoods have less access to open landscapes or high-quality green space.

It is urgent and critical that structural and political changes are made to address the inequality and neglect that lead to environmental and spatial injustice. Nature will mean different things to different cultures, but the mainstream stereotype and representation of nature in the UK as a white, middle-class, luxury pursuit is a fallacy and excludes people both from the experience of spending time in the living world and from the multitude of health and well-being benefits it can offer.

Nature is for everyone. Birds are for everyone. Digging holes and finding worms are for everyone. Looking for foxes and badgers is for everyone. Pond-dipping is for everyone. Climbing trees is for everyone. Swimming in rivers is for everyone. Spending time in calming, restorative natural environments is for everyone. The infinite variety of the world is for everyone. Nature *is* everyone. It mustn't be kept in the margins of our children's lives.

An intimate relationship with the rest of nature will enhance your life in so many ways. It will offer your children much more than society gives it credit for. A meaningful kinship with other beings can root children in the earth and offer both a steady footing and membership of a wider family for the rest of their lives. An inner stillness, peace and calm can be found in the natural world, as well as spontaneous moments of joy and excitement. For both children and adults, the scientific evidence is now unequivocal: a connection with nature is linked to better mental and physical health.

You will find ideas in this book for parents and caregivers, no matter how much time you have available. Sometimes a ten-minute walk or a roam in a few metres' radius is the perfect amount. We know it can be difficult to find moments to get out with children in our modern world of pressures, responsibilities and worries. Parents may be experiencing stress, and free time is not easy to come by. But no matter what your situation, or where you live, or how much nearby nature you have available, we hope you'll find this a practical guide to empower your children to love the natural world. At the back of the book you will find a Resources section (see page 211), which will help you expand, nurture and deepen your wild life.

Chapters Two and Three lay the foundations of our philosophy and relate mostly to babies, toddlers and the pre-school years of childhood. Chapters Four to Seven are for all ages. Chapter Eight is directed towards older children, aged ten, eleven or twelve. The final part, Chapter Nine, ends with a call to action for rewilding childhood. We have finished with a look outwards at our present society, because we think children urgently need more connection with the living world. We've analysed where we think our culture needs to progress and evolve, by giving nature experiences back to children, which should be a birthright: a chance to run through long grass until their heart beats like a drum, to climb a tree and become a bird or a squirrel, to paddle in rivers looking for minnows.

You will find reasons why children need nature peppered through the book, drawn from my (Lucy's) research into the scientific evidence for nature connection and human health. I have studied this for a number of years. More specifically, I've picked out the most compelling and pertinent research about children and nature that I could find: from the polymath Edith Cobb's study of creative expression and the genius of childhood, to scientists studying ADHD (attention deficit hyperactivity disorder) in children and the effect of nature; from the writings of leading global environmental educators responding to the creeping enclosure of children indoors, to cultural depictions of children's relationship with nature, ranging from Walt Whitman's poetry to *Hey Duggee*. To find out why nature is important to children, and why children aren't getting enough time outdoors, I interviewed teachers, outdoor educators, street-play and access activists and primary-school children.

The Nature Seed will suggest a different way of seeing your environment – finding awe in the cracks of the pavement and magic on a walk around the block. You don't have to travel to the mountains or the ocean to find moments of wonder. They exist right outside your door. Nor do you need any special clothes or kit. All you need is your senses.

Children have an innate curiosity about living things. From the beginning of their lives, they are drawn to other forms of life and their shapes, patterns and textures: the squelching mud, the crawling insects, the smooth conker, the spongy moss. We have observed this in our own children – the immediate kicking of legs and squealing of a baby who sees a dog running or a horse shaking its mane. The personhood given to woodlice on the street corner. The fearless wonder in letting a bumblebee walk onto a small hand.

As teenagers and then adults, we often lose the thrill and interest that we felt while spending time in nature. We forget what's out there: the colours and sounds and scents. We may not know the names of trees or the birds that live within them; or how the toil of insects leads to the

food on our plate; or how trees clean the air that we breathe. Some of us may never even have been exposed to the outdoors very much in the first place. By adulthood, being 'in nature' can feel like being on an alien planet. So the

Even young babies and toddlers can explore the textures of the natural world

idea of imparting knowledge or a love of nature to our own children might be intimidating because we don't know what to do or what to say.

But there is an urgent need and longing to reconnect with the living world, and perhaps you feel it, too. We can see this in the growth of Forest School and outdoor nurseries; in the battles to save street trees and protect woodlands; in doctors and health professionals who are recognising that connection with nature for all people is a cornerstone of good human mental and physical health; in the rising up of communities concerned about the climate and biodiversity crisis. There is a growing desire to rewild childhood, which has never been more critical.

Who are you, and why should we listen to you?

I – Lucy – am an author, journalist, mother of three and keen naturalist. I wrote a book called *Losing Eden* about the relationship between nature and mental health. My first book, *Foxes Unearthed*, was about the ambivalent relationship between people in Britain and the fox. I write about science, health and the environment for a number of publications, such as the *Guardian* and the BBC. I'm particularly interested in how the human mind intersects with the natural environment.

I live in a town in Hampshire, after many years in London, and spend as much time as possible in nature with my children, Evie (four), Max (two) and baby Gabriel. I'm happiest when sitting beside a river with dragonflies, damselflies and my family, before a swim in the cool water and a search for caddis-fly larvae and perhaps the chance of a kingfisher rocketing through. I'm drawn to nature because it's never boring. I love the way the forests and the woodlands and the ocean and the rivers change from minute to minute, and there's always something to learn more about or discover. I also love the constancy of nature, and I have found communion with the wild to be profoundly therapeutic. I'm addicted to awe and wonder.

Ken lives in Essex and is the manager of Tower Hamlets Cemetery Park in London. He has worked full-time in nature conversation since 2000 and has more than two decades of experience of working with children in natural spaces, including running Forest School: child-led, supported risk-taking sessions of hands-on experience, play and exploration in a natural area, ideally a woodland. He has spent his whole life in the living world, and his goal as a child was to turn his love of the natural world into a career. He loves people, and sharing his love of the outdoors through nature walks, bat walks or wild-food walks. He is the father of Elsie (eight) and Amelia (ten), with whom he has spent many thousands of hours outdoors. I first met him on a bat walk at the Cemetery Park, where he made and served a delicious foraged nettle soup, for which you'll find the recipe later in the book (see page 159).

As you will see, we are advocates for engaging with nature in an easy, free, child-led way that doesn't require any particular equipment, tools or clothes (although a waterproof jacket and shoes can be handy, and a back-carrier for a baby or toddler can make longer walks or adventures more possible). We love finding the magic in local, everyday nature and the interconnections around us in the urban neighbourhoods that we inhabit. We feel strongly – based on both our research and our experience

– that children need nature, more so than our society currently allows for or encourages.

Does it really matter if more children can recognise the golden arches of McDonald's than an oak leaf?
Forming deep and sustaining bonds with the living world in childhood – and adulthood – is unique and important. There are many reasons for this, but, at this point, we'll boil it down to three.

First, evidence shows that spending time in nature as a child is more likely to lead to a relationship with nature in adulthood, even if you go through a dormancy period, as many people do in their teens. It is the key determining factor in a continuing relationship with nature, and therefore with all the ensuing health and well-being benefits.

Second, a relationship with nature is linked with pro-environmental behaviours. We can only love what we know, and we can only protect what we love. At a time of climate breakdown and biodiversity loss, nurturing children's innate interest in and love of the wider world is a crucial act of parenthood and education. It should go without saying, but this is the case for both sexes. Researchers have suggested that if girls are not given the same opportunities for environmental exploration and play outdoors as boys, their 'confidence and ability to cope with environmental matters are likely to be undermined'.*

Third, as we've touched on, connection with the rest of nature is good for our bodies and minds. Evidence shows

* Gary Paul Nabhan and Stephen Trimble, *The Geography of Childhood: Why Children Need Wild Places*, Beacon Press, 1994, p. 72.

The wilder part of the garden appeals to Max as he learns to crawl

that children who spend more time in nature are less likely to have mental-health problems in later life. Being outside in nature is associated with positive health outcomes, from more creative play to social and cognitive development; from a reduction of ADHD symptoms to better psychological health and the building of confidence and resilience. We recover from stress more completely and quickly in a natural environment compared to a built environment. As the vast majority of people live in urban areas, where stress-related illnesses are on the rise, a relationship with restorative places will become ever more crucial. Rates of autoimmune diseases, such as asthma, eczema and Type 1 diabetes, are also rising in the Western world, and research from Finland suggests that greener play areas boost children's immune systems within a month.* Nearby nature can reduce stress in more vulnerable children who have faced hardship.

There are aspects, too, that are harder to measure in a lab. Beauty, for example, delight, imagination and, crucially, freedom. It isn't easy for children to feel free in the twenty-first century. The roaming area of children has decreased by 90 per cent since the 1970s. Children are trapped indoors by traffic on the roads. The dominance of cars means that street play is mostly a memory. Health-and-safety concerns, and fears of abduction and strangers, have led to a time when the accolade of the 'World's Worst Mom' goes to the American Lenore Skenazy, who let her nine-year-old son ride the New York subway on his own.

* Damian Carrington, 'Greener play areas boost children's immune systems, research finds', *The Guardian*, 14 October 2020, www.theguardian.com/environment/2020/oct/14/greener-play-areas-boost-childrens-immune-systems-research-finds.

When I talk to my grandmother about her 1930s childhood in the suburbs of London, how much has changed becomes clear. She talks about exploring open land and a big mound of earth surrounded by water called The Moat, which was past the fence of their garden. She and her brother – with no parental supervision – spent hours there, alone, wading, finding great crested newts, coots, moorhens, frogs and frogspawn.

We're not suggesting a return to the 1930s, but can we, as a society, find more of an indoor–outdoor balance to go with our work–life balance?

Over the years of working with children, Ken has noticed that when children are in nature, they feel free and thus act freely. There is the chance to expand and be themselves. Nature offers the ability to breathe, in both a physical and emotional sense. Walking and running and exploring and rolling and creeping through wide-open spaces without barriers or obstacles is an important part of childhood and, indeed, of human life on Earth. We spent 99 per cent of our evolutionary history in contact with the natural world, and evolutionary perspectives – such as E. O. Wilson's 'biophilia hypothesis', which posits the idea that there is a genetic disposition and need within us to commune with nature – suggest this is why there remains a worldwide tendency to be drawn towards landscapes that resemble the wide-open savannahs of our erstwhile habitats. We know, for example, that prehistoric youngsters probably spent even more time climbing trees than adults did. Anthropologists in New Hampshire studied the almost-complete foot of a two-and-a-half-year-old *Australopithecus afarensis*, an early human, and found she had slightly ape-like feet, for grabbing onto the branches of trees.

This affiliation to space and trees and wild pockets of vegetation is something I've noticed with my young children. When my son Max started to walk, his sense of glee was palpable as he waddled as far as he could across a field or beach, relishing the space and freedom, or wandered off to explore the half of our garden that's left wild – early moments of autonomy. He often gravitates to this patch, where sweet pea and clematis and aquilegia have created a kind of tiny urban jungle. There are little areas to hide and crouch in and different shapes to touch, from the hard early plums and different lengths of twigs, to the soft clocks of the dandelion.

How can nature connection affect the relationship between parent and child?

Sharing the joys of nature with children can be an intimate and bonding part of your life together. The child will show you something they've seen; you share something you've found; and this continuous to and fro builds a shared emotional experience, stand-out memories and a hobby that could last a lifetime. By being out together in a different world, following both your mutual and separate enthusiasms, other distractions are limited. I find I'm less likely to be tempted to check or scroll on my phone. It's symbiotic, and that adult sense of disenchantment and cynicism dissolves when met with the fresh, enthusiastic joy of a child seeing something for the first time. My children are just as often my guide as I am theirs.

When Evie turned four, she became an adept beetle-spotter. Whenever we walked in the woods she'd spot different beetles in the grass and mud that we would never have noticed, being a metre or more above her. We soon realised that the underside of the beetle carapace was a brilliant turquoise green or blue, depending on how the sunlight shone. It was a moment of shared discovery – well, her teaching me, really – and awe that we've built on together ever since. At moments of high emotion, I've found that making a fairy room in the trunk of a tree, with sticks for the walls, leaves for the beds, acorn cups for the bowls, and so on, can be a calming, soothing activity.

On a day out, Ken, Amelia and Elsie stumbled across an emergence of baby frogs by chance. While choosing a picnic spot, Amelia decided to check out a moss-covered bank on the other side of a thin, shallow stream. She suddenly noticed an abundance of tiny froglets hopping on the bank. They were the only people on the planet with front-row seats witnessing these new creatures taking their first hops on land. It was a moment of serendipity and magic.

We want to give you the confidence to lead your child into the living world (and we feel confident that they will start leading you as well: you'll never see as many insects as when out and about with a child who comes up to your knee). For many of us, the outdoors is flat 'green wallpaper', to use the phrase of writer and botanist Robin Wall Kimmerer, but once we start spending time looking and seeing, touching and sniffing, then the knowing deepens and it becomes easier, automatic. The world comes to life with infinite dimensions, together.

By planting the seed of this process, and discovering and adventuring in the wild together, you will pass to your

Amelia and Elsie potion-making in a tree hole in Danbury, Essex

child a lifelong gift that is never static or terminal. There is always more to find and discover in the natural world. It is a bottomless treasure trove for the curious.

Spending time in nature is also an activity in which both adult and child can reap similar and shared emotional experiences. You might not enjoy building Lego or arts and crafts, but it's likely you will respond to the beauty, awe and peace found in the natural world, and to the mental and physical health benefits. The evidence suggests that you'll feel less stressed being in nature with your children, and your well-being and even your productivity may increase.

We want our children to be happy and secure. We want to leave them with an appreciation and love of nature – a place they will go to for fun, pleasure, strength, sustenance and comfort, and with their own children, if they have them. Spending time in the living world costs nothing, can last for minutes or all day, and you can do it in all weathers. It's exciting and dynamic, as the world responds to the time of day and year, anchored in this shared, synergistic experience between parent and child. And, of course children also sleep better after playing in the fresh air.

What if I don't know anything about ecology or what to do in nature?

Don't worry. You don't need to know anything about ecology, or what species is what.

An important element of engaging your children with nature is your own curiosity. What do *you* find beautiful or interesting? Butterflies? Foraging for wild garlic? Moss? Explore what you find wondrous. The more excited you are by the natural world, the more your wonder will be infectious. And the more you look, the more you will see. There are lots of great apps around to help you identify plants and trees and mushrooms.

Think back to your earliest, happiest memory of spending time in nature. It might be pond-dipping at school, or looking for crabs in rockpools on holiday, or making dens in the woods. You might not have spent much time in nature as a child, but have good memories of outdoor play: football in the local park or watching the sparrows on your street. Perhaps you can remember the meditative satisfaction of creating a home-made daisy chain. Or the simple calm of lying under a tree at break-time and looking up at the branches and leaves on a warm day. Or the plants in the playground that you'd mindlessly pick and smell. Chances are you might still be drawn to the same aspects.

Ken's earliest childhood memory is feeding the red ants that had a colony under the single stone step of his garden path:

I would always share with the ant colony part of my jam ring or Bourbon biscuit that I got most days as a late-afternoon snack. It always impressed me how the ants found the biscuit piece, and how the biscuit would eventually be smothered by hundreds of ants, as they each marched to be part of the biscuit banquet. It did disappoint me, though, that my gift never seemed to be fully appreciated, as I always ended up with an ant bite at the top of my legs and thighs as I sat and watched them. How very ungrateful of them – or was I getting an ant kiss?

I was a keen collector of ladybirds, aphids, snails – anything I could gather up and stick into a plastic blue-lidded insect box. I roamed the bushes and shrubs of the garden, picking up ladybirds with my fingers and laying them on the leaves I'd collected for food. I remember the pungent smell of the orange liquid they would emit on my hands, in defence.

But some of my favourite memories involve my parents. On holiday in France in the summer, we would sometimes go out for a meal in the evening. I loved the chips and fizzy drinks and the pinball machine, but the highlight happened on the way back. My father would stop the car by the side of the road, in the middle-of-nowhere countryside, and we'd step into the velvety darkness. It was soft and quiet and warm. I could smell the musk of the earth, the heat of the soil cooling down after an August day. The stars were bright, but the main course was the sound. Crickets and frogs letting rip – a symphony of staccato ribbits. The landscape pulsed. More stars appeared in the purple dark. I saw 'my' stars: the three in a row that seemed to follow me around. There was something about being out after dark (rare), the abundance of animals (thrilling) and the fact it was my father showing it to us that made it extra-special.

In terms of what you can do in nature, this book is filled with activities and ideas drawn from Ken's extensive expertise and his time working with kids in nature. We've got you covered.

Chapter Two

Wildlife in the Home

In summer we consider the whine of
the mosquito, the secrecy of the spider,
the temper of the wasp – who among us
could love you? Who could love even one
of you, bearing your poisons and your pain
into the heavy summertime air? We could.
We could love you if we remind ourselves
that no creature is made up only of poison,
that no life is only a source of irritation
or pain.

Margaret Renkl, 'Praise Song for the Unloved Animals',
New York Times, 27 May 2019

Lucy: What's nature, Evie?
Evie (aged three): Trees ... spiders ... leaves ...
birds ... Me, I am nature.

It might seem strange to start a book about children and
nature inside. But we will start in the home because it's
where your children may have their early experiences of
wildlife. A spider in the bath. A mouse on the kitchen floor.
A crane fly stumble-skittering up a curtain. As mentioned
in the first chapter, we now spend 95–9 per cent of our time
indoors. Many of us live in flats without gardens or parks

and woods close by. That means plenty of opportunities to engage with nature in the home.

The idea that 'nature' is something 'out there', a kind of chocolate-box, picture-postcard image of species that are aesthetically pleasing – pretty flowers, clement weather, solely wildlife that appeal to our culturally influenced value judgements – is simply not what the living world is. Mosquitoes are just as much nature as bluebells are. Rats are just as much nature as puffins are. Of course a wasp sting is a pain, but no animal exists solely to irritate or hurt us. Every species has multiple connections with other animals and is, like us, simply trying to survive. The natural world is within us. When we know a little more about the wider ecology in which we live, it can become marvellous and psychedelic.

Now this book will be more about getting out into the living world, but how we relate to and perceive the animals that live among us is part of fostering a connection. And we promise you: there are opportunities for awe and wonder in the home. Sharing a bathroom with a bright lemon-yellow brimstone moth for a few weeks one summer became an everyday burst of joy for me: observing its intricate brown-and-white marbled markings and the concentrated citrus fluff on its head first thing in the morning and at bathtime.

If we can get past any received wisdom about 'pests', there are also opportunities for experiencing wildlife simply as it is, without the overlay of aesthetic influence and Romantic notions of nature, which shape the way we interpret the outside world. There aren't any poems by William Wordsworth or paintings by J. M. W. Turner of spiders or roaches, after all. Our proximity to wildlife indoors, then, can burst the modern cultural illusion of human separateness.

While researching this chapter, I sat with Evie, who was then three, to read an old 1970s Collins *Guide to Wild Life in House and Home*. It's a very seventies-looking book, all muted browns, oranges and slate-greys. On the first plate there was an abundance of intricate drawings of woodlice, centipedes, worms, slugs, scorpions, harvestmen and spiders close up. It showed details: the ridges and bumps on the woodlouse carapace and the hairs on the spider's legs. I love invertebrates, especially spiders, but I noticed that my very first reaction to seeing *a lot* of these creatures on the page up close was a primal, instinctual disgust. Evie's reaction, however, was simple amazement. She spotted the spiders she sometimes finds in the bathroom, and the woodlice she loves, especially when they curl up into a perfect round ball. She didn't utter any sense of fear or revulsion. She wanted to look at each invertebrate in turn, considering their legs and structures and heads and claws.

I realised that even though I say I love insects, I'm influenced by a society that sees all creepy-crawlies as 'pests' and essentially wants to eradicate bugs who are in 'our' space. Of course this is an over-reaction. Very few of the bugs who share our homes can bite or sting. None, in the UK, can do any real harm to the vast majority of people.

Young children know that we are all part of the natural world. They easily relate to insects and creatures as 'he' and 'she' and 'friends'. A child's first pets are often woodlice and ladybirds. Children love animals, and it's often the adult perception of nature that gradually influences that innate affection out of them, or their peers at nursery or school. In an episode of *Hey Duggee*, a favourite TV show in our house, one of the characters, Norrie, is terrified of a spider and in the early part of the episode she and the others scream every time they see it. For a while my daughter would imitate this reaction, learning that spiders were something to be afraid of. The rest of the episode thankfully takes a more level-headed stance, with the characters realising the spider is actually 'tiny' and working together to find it a new home in the doll's house, but the seed had been planted that spiders were, in some way, enemies. This is no small thing: in my interviews with teachers and environmental educators, fear of creepy-crawlies was cited as a major barrier to children connecting with the natural world. Children who believe bugs are frightening are less keen to engage with natural play, such as looking under logs and touching plants and trees. Finding a spider in a wellington boot might put a group of children off wanting to go outside at all. The trend for building 'bug hotels' – shelters for insects – in schools can help children get over the phobia, I'm told.

Insects, the largest group in the animal kingdom, are of course extremely beneficial to us. And we are a lot more stitched into the rest of nature than we realise. The beings that live in our guts influence our health and how we feel. We even have arthropods living on our faces. The microscopic mite *Demodex* eats, mates and finally dies in your pores, follicles and sebaceous glands. We are never, then, truly alone, but simply interconnected with all manner of life.

It's important to observe our behaviour at home or outside and be conscious of ways in which we might react to a wasp, say, or a spider. Obviously wasps can be annoying and no one wants a wasp to sting their child, but they are not the enemy. If a child's first experience of a spider or moth is a parent wanting to swat and kill it as quickly as possible, it's not exactly going to sell spiders or moths to the child as other beings to respect or protect. We are the greatest influences on our children and if we communicate unwarranted, mindless fear and disgust for insects, for example, it's likely to limit the child's growing interest. How we talk about other creatures matters. A relationship of love and kinship with nature is cultivated by the way we consider and perceive other species.

This isn't to say that emotions of fear and disgust aren't valid or going to arise, or that there is any 'right' way to feel about 'nature'. Disgust might be a common emotion when faced with aspects of the natural world, whether it's cleaning out a maggot-filled bin or looking at the bloody carcass of a dead bird. What prevents a response from then cutting off future experiences of being outside among other beings is letting the emotion come and go, rise and fall. I'd rather give my children the chance to see things that might invoke disgust, and to embrace the complexity of the natural world in all its weird glory – and the mixture of emotions it triggers – than pretend it doesn't exist or close the door on it. You can direct a child's jumpiness at the sight of a spider to a place of learning, curiosity or even empathy.

Are you saying that I should live with wasps or mice in my home?

No one *wants* rats or mice putting their feet up in front of the television, or clothes-eating moths in the wardrobe (although almost all species of moth won't touch your jumpers). We are simply cautioning against bringing in binary ideas around 'good' or 'bad' species because it may limit your child's view of the wider world. There are facts about rats and mice that might be interesting to children. Did you know that mice have lived alongside humans for up to 15,000 years, from even before the dawn of agriculture? Or that rats are highly intelligent and have been trained to give high-fives and fetch a ball?

Of course a few species, such as rats, can't be accommodated indoors – humane ways to repel rodents include keeping food stored, surfaces clean and blocking up holes – but relaxing about animals in the home that aren't going to eat your stuff, or bring any risk of disease, can be rewarding and can challenge the idea that nature, still, is something either to be subdued and destroyed or idealised and romanticised.

Being stung by a wasp can be painful of course, but wasps – or indeed any invertebrate – aren't malevolent, despite what certain sections of the press ('Killer wasps!', 'Murder hornets!') might want you to think. Some people are genuinely phobic of spiders, but for most of us our fear is a mixture of learned behaviours, cultural influence and perhaps an innate 'biophobia' of certain animals that would have posed a threat to our survival as a species. There may be a primal, instinctive fear reaction built into our genetic inheritance that lasts in our nature-deprived modern environments.

Can we choose to see spiders as helpful residents with important jobs, such as eating mosquitoes and other flies? Or how about making up names for the moths and spiders

A butterfly hospital created by Amelia and Elsie with their friends outside our home, to help a lethargic Red Admiral

in your house? We've found that giving the massive spider that lives in the bathroom the moniker 'Johnny Big Bones' adds a certain amusing familiarity to his presence.

We don't want to romanticise nature. Nature doesn't exist to be beautiful and astonishing for us. Multiple elements and species in the natural world *are* beautiful and astonishing and even romantic, but it's not a perfect sunny theme-park. We had to tweezer four ticks off Max in his first year, and I can't pretend I wanted to look at those ticks with any measure of awe and wonder. Nor do I fancy befriending the rats that sometimes appear in the garden.

But they're all part of the web of life. And we believe that having a full, rich, honest, authentic sense of the rest of nature will enhance and deepen your children's lives.

There are other reasons to accommodate animals who might wander in. If you get the chance to sit and watch a spider weave a web, it's a magical experience. If it's in the corner of your living room, well, you've got a living spell, a pellucid dream-catcher, a supernatural embroidery right there. But you'll also witness the brutality of nature. Animals kill each other. They are desperately trying to survive. With our move away from nature, we've buffered ourselves against the reality of our wider environment. We're not experiencing the dynamics of the living world on a day-to-day basis. Interactions in the home can give us a glimpse of the reality of our world and opportunities for interesting conversations about interconnectedness.

Of course you can always just put the insects gently outside. One day Evie, then three, said to a roaming crane fly, 'I don't like daddy-long-legs, I don't want them near me.' She was painting and didn't want an insect in her space. She started to get very annoyed when another one turned up. 'Daddy-long-legs, you're not my best friend!' she cried. Fair enough. What to do? Well, we simply let the crane fly crawl onto our hand and put it elsewhere, as kindly as possible, without vilifying or demonising it. If something similar happens, how about considering telling your child how spiders and other invertebrates would once have lived in caves, among early humans. Now, however, our homes are their caves, where they find lots of food and shelter, away from bad weather. It's no wonder they want to live with us.

What's the wider problem here? Who cares if a few spiders get squished?

In my interviews with people working with children and outdoor education, it became very clear that fear of bugs is a major problem in connecting more kids with nature.

The more eco-alienation creeps into our society – as habitats are destroyed and species decline, and children are given fewer opportunities to engage with the living world – the more it seems clear that our anthropocentric imaginings are driving the divide. It seems as if anything that is in our designated space we call 'pest' or 'vermin' and try to eradicate. The problem is that our designated space is now everywhere, bar a few oases of nature reserves across the country, as we can see in the plummeting populations of other species.

One of the ways we could evolve past this hallucination that humans are superior is by considering the rights of other species, and the fact that other animals are simply trying to find shelter and feed their babies, just like us, and their right to exist is intrinsic.

Much of this book will be about wonder and awe and beauty, and the pleasurable experiences that we can take from spending time in nature, but we also want to suggest thinking about a reciprocal relationship with the natural world. How can we live in reciprocity with our animal kinfolk? We are given so much from the Earth, from clean air to our food, to calmness and beauty. What can we give back?

Education in the home is a perfect starting point for doing away with ideas that some species are good and others are bad, on the basis of how they benefit us. We tend to categorise spiders and flies and – stay with us – fleas and mites as 'not nature', but they are. Children know this, before it becomes socialised out of them. As we grow older and enter adulthood, we forget that the 'pests' that are killed so that food and flowers can grow are part of the web of life in which we are all interconnected. We only live because of insects.

Often the most important question may be: How can we move out of the way and allow children to have a full and unlimited relationship with the living world?

KEN'S IDEAS AND ACTIVITIES

For most children I've met, including my own two, there is an inbuilt curiosity and wonder about all things, especially towards the unfamiliar and things that look so different from humans. Wildlife fulfils that criteria! Be amazed by the fact that creatures can fly, make webs, have defensive organs such as venomous bites or a sting; look more closely at their markings, colours and body shape. If you can do so safely and without harm to you or the creature, capture it, look at it and then let it go. Everything has the right to life and, in my mind, the default position should be always to release wildlife back outside, and not dead, as squishy remains to be cleaned off the bottom of a shoe, slipper or flip-flop. I'm confident that most adults know that rescuing wildlife is the proper response, but our concerns and fears can often override our rational side.

Here are some common species that you'll come across in and around your home.

Birds

Extremely diverse, plump and covered in feathers, these flying avian dinosaurs are attracted to feeding stations and birdbaths. House sparrows and starlings are most likely to share your home and nest in your roof, entering between the roof tiles and guttering. Other birds use drainpipes, ventilation grilles and even a hole in your house wall. I've known robins to nest in an old paint pot. The RSPB (Royal Society for the Protection of Birds) website has many resources to help you identify them by sight, and to train your ears to recognise bird songs.

Beyond feeding our feathered friends, you could consider making (or buying) and then erecting your own bird nest box. Many birds, such as robins, sparrows, starlings, wrens and blue tits, will use a nest box. It's a great autumn and winter activity to have nesting opportunities ready for the approaching spring. These are often best placed between north and east, to allow the adults to incubate the eggs and not be affected by the sun's warmth or by wind. They should be placed high – the exact height is dictated by the birds you want to attract – and installed with a slight tilt forward to shed the rain. Also put the nest box well out the way of any inquisitive pet cats, and make sure there's a clear, uncluttered flight path to the nest-box entrance. If your local green space or garden can limit the mowing regime on a patch of grass close to where you have placed nest boxes, and you have a small pool of water and some logs, these wildlife refuge areas will provide the essential invertebrates, such as caterpillars for the adult birds to collect and feed to their developing chicks.

Moths

With more than 2,500 species in the UK, moths are divided into macro moths (around 900 species) and micro moths, or 'little brown jobs', as experts like to call them. These smaller moths can be difficult to identify.

Many moths fly at night, but not all – there are many easily recognisable day-flying species. And moths perform the same function as butterflies, visiting flowers to drink nectar and, in the process, pollinating them. There are several species that you may find flying into your home or see in your garden or local green space.

One that I see regularly pop up on my social-media news feed, to be identified, is the poplar hawk-moth, a large, oddly shaped and not easily disturbed moth. Its strange appearance is because, when at rest, it holds its hind wings forward in front of its forewing.

How about those unusual moths that look like a capital T when they're at rest? These are called plume moths and they are common across the UK. The distinctive T-shape is because at rest the moth rolls its wings up tightly.

Finally there's the striking six-spot burnet moth, which is black with red spots and can be found throughout the UK. It's brightly marked as a warning

Mating poplar hawk-moths

Plume moth at rest

to predators that it is poisonous. When attacked, these moths release hydrogen cyanide, which is a chemical compound metabolised from their larval food-plant, bird's-foot trefoil.

Ants, bees and wasps

Bothersome and unwanted at a picnic or barbecue, bees and wasps are often dispatched quickly with a death-blow – or a generous application of killing powder, if you're an ant colony. In July or August people will often notice hundreds of flying ants in the sky, usually the black ant *Lasius niger*, and as a result this annual spectacle of reproduction is often accompanied by ill-informed 'Flying Ant Day' posts on social media, and by articles in national papers describing the event as an invasion and providing suggestions on how to dispatch the ants. People may then take a trip to the shop to get insecticide products to deal with what they may consider an unpleasant nuisance. The flying ants are young queens and males appearing for their nuptial flight. They mate in flight, and the queens are much larger than the males and can often be seen flying with a male attached. The larger number of ants appearing in a short time period is to increase the chance that a queen will mate with a male from a different colony. Once mated, the queen must then begin a colony of her own. Ants in the ground, or flying, pose no risk or danger to humans and actually benefit the soil, aerating it and recycling nutrients, and they are a vital food resource for many species of birds.

Usually at the end of summer people are driven inside by the irritation of persistent wasps. This is because the adult wasps are no longer being fed the sugar-rich spit from the colony's larvae, and so they are tempted by and attracted to the many sweet treats eaten by humans outside. This increased awareness and presence of 'bothersome' wasps will lead to ill-informed social-media posts, defending the bumblebees and honeybees and describing them as cute, cuddly and fluffy makers of honey. Everything wasp-like is imbued with a bad reputation and is described as skinny, mean and good-for-nothing. Bees and wasps are important pollinators, but wasps have the added benefit of being predators and detritivores (eating decomposing plants and animals). Adult wasps hunt other invertebrates, such as caterpillars and spiders, to feed to their larvae back at their nest. Adults only feed on sugars and will consume nectar and unwanted fallen fruit later in the year, needing these sugars to fuel them. Wasps are natural pest controllers, keeping ecosystems balanced and cleaning up the world.

We would be poorer without them. When admiring bees and wasps, it's always best to stay still. Please add wasps to your list of gardener's friends.

Spiders

Probably the least loved of all our wildlife, and considered ugly with their eight long legs and big bum, spiders are guilty of making many people feel fearful and uncomfortable. But spiders are natural pest controllers, helping to keep ecosystems in balance, and are good indicators of the health of an ecosystem. On a dewy morning in short grass you could see hundreds of tiny sheet webs made by money spiders, and September brings the fascinating orb weavers with their intricately made webs. Have you seen black-and-white zebra jumping spiders on a brick wall?

With their big eyes and great vision, these spiders will look at you. They're able to map the terrain where prey is

Female garden spider waiting for prey to fall victim to her intricate web

Left: Crab spider lying in wait for a visiting insect on a scabious flower
Right: Zebra jumping spider

in sight, so they can decide the best point to leap from, to catch their quarry. This could actually mean they have to move across the landscape, losing sight of their prey before they are able to reach the ideal jumping point to hunt from. How about crab spiders that lie in wait for an insect to visit a flower? Not all spiders employ webs to catch prey, but they deserve our admiration and interest.

Butterflies

Of the fifty-nine butterfly species in the UK, fifty-seven are resident. These beautiful insects are an important part of the UK's wildlife and a significant indicator for the health of the ecosystem. This is because of their short life cycles, their limited dispersal ability, their close reliance on the weather and climate and their food-plant specialisation. They also pollinate plants.

Butterflies will visit any garden with suitable nectar plants, such as buddleia, comfrey, crocus, foxglove, geranium, lavender and marjoram, to name but a few. Regular home visitors tend to be the brightly coloured peacocks, with eyespots on the fore and hind wings.

They often rest with their wings closed but, when disturbed, will flash open their wings, which look like eyes and briefly startle a predator, giving the butterfly time to escape. Another visitor is the comma, so called for the white comma-shaped marking on the underwing. Look out for an orange butterfly with black spots and a torn outer-edge appearance to its wings. Males often bask with their

wings fully open and will fly up to chase away anything that flies overhead.

The reason we see these butterflies in our homes is, first, because they may accidentally fly in on a warm day when doors or windows are open; and, second, because several species of butterfly hibernate as adults. These species look for sheltered places, and our homes make a good alternative to a log pile or tree hollow. When we heat our homes for the winter, butterflies will wake

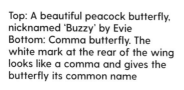

Top: A beautiful peacock butterfly, nicknamed 'Buzzy' by Evie
Bottom: Comma butterfly. The white mark at the rear of the wing looks like a comma and gives the butterfly its common name

up from hibernation. This isn't good for the butterfly, as it's using up the body fuel it made to see it through the winter. I would suggest gently collecting the butterfly and putting it somewhere cold and dark outside, away from potential predators; or keep it safe until there's a sunny day with a temperature of around 10° Celsius and release it outside to find its own suitable place to hibernate.

Ladybirds

Ladybirds are the gardener's friend because they eat aphids, which are considered plant pests and will reduce the overall health of the plant. Live adult ladybirds were being sold on eBay at the beginning of the Covid-19 pandemic for

Seven-spot ladybird

around £30 for fifty adults (and in some cases for much more, for many fewer adults) because of demand and an increased interest in growing our own food.

Ladybirds are a favourite among children and adults alike. Their bright markings mean they're always swiftly gathered up by a child to be held, and I've witnessed children arguing over whose turn it is next to hold these vibrant-coloured beetles. All ladybirds in the UK hibernate and, in the absence of natural sheltered places, you may find them clustering to hibernate in our homes, especially along windowsills. The adults that you see at this time won't naturally reproduce until the following year when the weather is warmer and there is food. As we warm our homes for the winter, we wake these beetles up from hibernating and they will begin to mate and lay eggs. This is potentially bad for them, as they're reproducing during a time of lean resources for them and their young, wasting stored energy and increasing the likelihood of dying, so please put them somewhere sheltered outside.

ACTIVITIES TO CELEBRATE THE WILDLIFE YOU SEE

Make a model spider or insect

Grab some Play-Doh or Blu-tack and make two balls for a spider, or three for an insect. Keep them as balls or mould them into different shapes and sizes to best represent what you saw, then gently stick each ball in a straight line, one behind the other. You can use bits of cocktail stick to help secure each body segment together, if you like. You can also use cocktail sticks or pipe cleaners for the legs. Where are the legs on a spider or insect? For spiders, the legs are growing from what we would describe as the head, while insects have their legs on the middle body segment, called the thorax. Spiders have eight legs, and insects have six.

Again use cocktail sticks or pipe cleaners to make the antennae for the insect's head, and for the appendages, or pedipalps, on the front of the spider's face. Pedipalps look a bit like an extra pair of legs on a spider, although they're often used like arms, to hold prey; they are also like antennae, helping the spider to sense objects that it encounters. In males, the pedipalps are used in mating to transfer sperm to female spiders. You can distinguish male from female spiders because a male spider's pedipalps are enlarged and look a bit like boxing gloves.

Decorate your insect or spider with other bits of coloured dough, or using felt tips to colour bits of Blu-tack. Feel free to embellish them with googly eyes, glitter or wings, which could be made from leaves that you find.

Copy the pattern of a bee or wasp
Grab a cardboard tube and, using paint, felt tips or pencils, draw and colour in the patterns you've seen on a bee or wasp. Are all the yellows the same, and are the stripes all the same thickness? Can you see spots or triangle markings?

Observe wood in the home
Find a piece of rotten wood and bring it home, then place it in any container you have. As the log dries out, wildlife will appear – be sure to put it somewhere suitable outside. Look closely at the log: what do you see? Black or coral-coloured spots could be a fungus; and if a piece is broken or bits

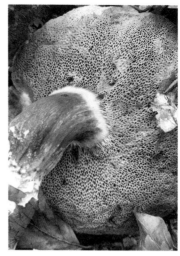

Boletes – a type of mushroom with sponge-like pores, found in woodland

flake off, you may see strands of white running through the wood. This is the mycelium, or vegetative parts, of a fungus stretching outwards in search of water and nutrients, which will be transported back to the fruiting body of the fungus so that it can grow. You may also see beetle larvae, woodlice, springtails, slugs, snails, centipedes and spiders. A whole world!

Grow some cornfield annuals

'Cornfield annuals' are easy-to-grow seed mixtures that are composed of such plants as poppy, cornflower, corn cockle, corn camomile and corn marigold. An annual is a plant that is sown, flowers and dies in one year. A shop-bought packet of seeds will usually contain one gram of seeds and will cost less than £4. This will be enough seeds for several recycled container-grown projects indoors. Many organisations sell or even give seeds away.

Any clean container, such as a butter tub or yoghurt pot, will do. If you have a garden, then a patch of well-lit, dug-over, level bare ground will work, too. If you're doing this outside, then a sowing rate of five grams of seed per square metre will work. Sow 'em, walk 'em in, water 'em and leave 'em: that will work fine. For your indoor container, fill it with soil/compost – any growing medium will do. The better the soil, the better the display of flowers, though. You can tell if you have good, healthy soil because it is often darker in colour (generally speaking, the darker the colour, the more organic matter it contains); it will be filled with earthworms and other soil-based and underground creatures; and if it takes five seconds or less for your soil to absorb a glass of water, then it is probably pretty good soil and is doing well.

Sprinkle your seeds evenly and sparingly across the top of the soil (you'll often have enough seed for more than one container). Gently brush your fingertips over the seeds to spread them out and give them the lightest of soil covering, then water them sparingly and place them somewhere with good natural light. Don't forget to water them often to help with germination, although you don't want the soil permanently wet. Bear in mind that these types of annuals normally thrive in bare open ground. Cornfield annual seeds are very quick and easy to grow, inexpensive and require minimal maintenance. They need access to good natural light. Germination can happen in seven to ten days and they'll provide a very colourful show in just a few months. The flowers will attract bees and butterflies.

Chapter Three

A Walk Around the Block

To see a World in a Grain of Sand
And a Heaven in a Wild Flower
Hold Infinity in the palm of your hand
And Eternity in an hour.

William Blake, 'Auguries of Innocence', 1803

When people become parents it can be a period of significant, joyful, sometimes uncomfortable transition. Aspects of early childhood that differ from the mores of adulthood in the industrialised West are time, pace and attention. In their first years, the time and pace of a child may be at odds with those of an adult in the working world. If your child wants to sit down and play with soil for a while, or jump on and off a tree stump indefinitely, it can feel quite difficult and strange to let go and be 'in the moment', instead of hurrying to the next thing.

Before we spent considerable time with young children, we may have been focused on getting things done: achieving, earning, being productive, getting from one place to another, finding ways to boost our happiness and self-esteem – all set to the rapid tempo of modern life. Our hyper-consumerist late-capitalist society confers on us the sense that time is money, and that there is always something to acquire or optimise. Pausing, slowing down, doing

Fennel spotted on an urban safari, on which Evie found myriad wildflowers and plants around a building site

little, watching: these are not attributes that our societies celebrate or really allow for (unless you're recovering from burnout). Our busyness seeps into the life of our children. An oft-discussed aspect of modern childhood is the 'overscheduled' child, ferried from football practice to dance lessons with a violin on her back, who hasn't enough downtime, or opportunities to be bored and make up her own activities or play.

Children are not born with this sense of accelerated productivity or to-do lists. A baby may sit and watch a bee for a while, engrossed in the way it moves, simply taking in its flight and its colours and listening to the sound. If an adult was spotted bending down on a street to observe the movement of a worm, he or she would get funny looks (we've been there).

In those early years, in the transition to parenthood (or that reminder of the planet of childhood, in grandparenthood or caregiving), going for a walk with a very young child can be a challenge to those who have been operating at a different pace. But it can also be a unique opportunity to slow down and notice the world around us. It can force us to pause and experience wonder vicariously – or directly. It testifies to both adults and children that there is deep value in the ordinary everyday facets of life (which, once you really look, aren't ordinary at all). It teaches us how to fall in love with nature again. It teaches us how to *see*.

One late-spring morning I was walking through our local nature patch, an urban cemetery with beautiful old yews, beech and larch. In spring it's filled with wild garlic, daffodils and snowdrops. In autumn conkers and acorns and pine cones drop to the ground and the maples and oaks change colour every day. On this visit Evie had just started walking. She stopped and stared at something. I was in a hurry and I wanted her to keep moving. But she was transfixed. I looked down and saw a standard May smorgasbord blur of wildflowers and weeds. *Meh!* I liked flowers, but I wasn't yet convinced that there were things to see that I didn't already perceive. And besides, we had to get somewhere. I hate being late. I looked away and took a step, to encourage Evie to follow me along the path. She stayed, watching, and I looked again. *Come on!* I took her hand to usher her along.

She wouldn't budge, so then, defeated, I stopped, looked and saw – truly saw – what Evie was seeing. Buttercups. Bright-yellow incandescent buttercups that glowed as if they were lit up with tiny bulbs against the deep-green grass. I bent down to look closer, next to her line of vision, to investigate why they looked so shiny and the yellowest yellow I'd ever seen. I'd forgotten how the inside petals of buttercups have a different texture from most flowers. They look like they're brushed with a gloss paint, or metallic varnish, which reflects the light of the sun.

It was a lesson in noticing and seeing: that the way we look means we don't often see what is actually there; that the more we look,

Daisies and buttercups in flower

and *how* we look, creates a different experience of life, beauty and activity.

What else could we be looking for?

Say you come across a patch of flowers in a local park or a front garden. Take a moment to look inside a flower. Go beyond what's on the immediate surface. If you look deeper, you'll see other colours and the

Oxeye daisy by a roadside. So beautiful, but so easy to walk past without noticing

features of reproductive parts, different shapes – possibly an earwig, if you're lucky. Show your child how to run the stamen through a honeysuckle flower so that a spherical drop of nectar sits on the end, perfect for a small, sugary drink. Or how snapdragons got their name: pinch the flowers together to turn the flower into a dragon snapping its jaws. Allow your eyes to adjust and reveal luminous green aphids or tweedy autumn spiders or smart soldier beetles.

Look down into the cracks in the pavement and marvel at the fractal sprays of the weeds. Be nosy and curious. If you can enjoy the walk from A to B, it will add a surprising new layer of interest and excitement to your everyday world. In the spring and summer I take Evie out on a 'wildflower safari' on our street. It's a busy urban road with very little noticeable life, trees, flowers or animal species. But, after combing the verges and margins by the building site

Sprays of weeds that are fractal in shape, which means they activate areas of the brain associated with calmness and relaxation

opposite, we come home with our basket full to the brim of colour and shapes: scarlet pimpernel, poppies, evening primrose, dandelions, bird's-foot trefoil, clover.

'Come forth into the Light of things, let Nature be your teacher,' wrote Wordsworth. After spending time with buttercups, for example, you might learn that the buttercup has not one but two flat layers in the epidermis: one at the top and the next separated by a gap of air. The smoothness of the structure reflects the light better than any other flower and that's why it glistens like solid gold. Buttercups were some of the earliest flowering plants and belong to a group that originated in the Cretaceous period, when the planet was dominated by dinosaurs. So when you look at buttercups, you're looking at a flower that dinosaurs would have seen, too. A relationship with wild plants and ancient trees gives a sense of time that fires the imagination and curiosity,

Scarlet pimpernel at a building site. These flowers open at certain times of day according to where the sun is

and places your human life in the natural order – among ancient oaks that live for hundreds of years, and mayflies who live for hours.

A year or so later Evie was drawn towards a bush with white flowers in the same cemetery. I'd always ignored this bush; it looked boring and municipal, but I was becoming slightly more patient. I was learning to slow down and realise that there was more out there than meets the eye. I didn't see dawdling and observing as a waste of time any more. I joined her next to the bush and saw it was crawling with an abundance of bees. It smelled like maple syrup and sounded like an orchestra of different buzzing tones. There were bees of varied species, as well as butterflies, moths and other flying insects. But it was only through stopping and taking the time to see that we entered this portal of wonder, a stone's throw from a busy road and a shopping mall.

Does this close-up noticing do anything for me?

In the early years of childhood, looking after children can feel repetitive, with the same routines every day, until a development happens. If you can access, however, the child's-eye view of the world and their fresh perception, there will be moments of childcare that are mind-bending. The living world is full of hallucinatory occurrences: things becoming other things, metamorphoses, life, death, chance, beauty, a different sense of time. If you can let go of adult preoccupations, the places you need to be, the emails you have to send, and slow down, it becomes more enjoyable for everyone. Sometimes it might involve deep breaths and a reminder that it's okay to pause.

Once you begin to see through a child's eyes, you will find enchantment in your everyday walks. Your street will come to life, as you notice different flowers, wild plants, lichens and moss, insects and birds. It's like a book becoming a theatrical show, as you learn who the different actors are, with the plants changing and moving, the wildlife bustling around, the colours and smells and sounds, life revealing itself, the everyday stories of multiple beings that we live alongside, even in the most ultra-urban locales. You don't need to be in a forest or by the sea to witness complex ecological societies or mind-blowing phenomena.

Spend some time watching a spider build its web, or bees moving around a lavender bush, and you realise how strange and marvellously bizarre the world we live in – and so often ignore – really is. And you don't need anything at all. No kit, no expertise, no knowledge. Just a slight change of attitude and pace. Let a walk and your observation take as long as they can, even if it's simply stopping for five minutes, or taking a ten-minute saunter in your local green space and mindfully observing the life that's around you. No expectations: what happens happens.

It can take a while to get into the practice of this. Our minds are filled with lists and worries. We have spent many years living in modern adult time, where being late makes us feel anxious, and our lives and activities are parcelled up into sections of the day. But we will benefit from a new perspective on time. It's definitely taught me to be more present and contemplative.

You might notice that there is something completely absorbed and instinctive about a baby watching the flowers of a sweet-chestnut tree fly in the wind, or listening to the susurration of a tree. It captures their attention entirely, even if just for a few moments. When my children were babies and I couldn't console their tears, I would take them to look at a tree, and they would usually calm and fixate on the motion of the moving branches and leaves. I spent many hours pushing a pram under trees, to expose them to this calming movement. Even if it was only for a minute, it was a relief for both of us.

Isn't it possible to get all this stuff through books and TV shows?

There is a philosophical idea, developed by the German philosopher Martin Buber, called the I-It versus the I-Thou. The I-It relationship sees an object (or tree, or person) as separate from oneself, and the relationship is one of utility. The I-Thou relationship sees the 'Thou' not as a separate object, but instead as a mutual being, with presence, inclusion and total attention, and without previous impressions or preconceptions. Buber talked about looking at a tree. 'It can also happen, if will and grace are joined, that as I contemplate the tree I am drawn into a relation, and the tree ceases to be an It,' he wrote.* We would add to will and grace that through childhood, and spending time with young children, it is possible to perceive the rest of the living world with a radical kind of directness and presentness.

This visceral, direct experience of nature matters. It can't be simulated by watching nature documentaries or by learning about biology and ecology in class. Our society

* Martin Buber, *I and Thou*, trans. Walter Kaufmann, Touchstone, 1996, p. 58.

Evie aged two, scouting around a wall covered in moss, lichen and wildflowers

tells us that it is enough to experience nature through the television or textbooks, but this leads to an impoverished experience of the living world. As much as the David Attenborough documentaries are wonderful, and there are proven mental-health benefits from experiencing nature through technology, if we only access the natural world through high-definition, high-budget, highly edited wildlife documentaries, aren't we lulled into a delusion of intimacy with other animals? Could it make spending time in ordinary natural areas seem less spectacular? A study from researchers in the US found that stimulated virtual nature can increase support for national parks and forests, but 'tends to cause people to devalue their emotional experience of local natural areas'.*

We need a balance of both. Without hands-on, direct involvement with the natural world, children lose that deep, sensual, multi-dimensional closeness and affinity. Our local worlds (and for many of us that will be urban environments) are filled with species that have adapted to our human landscapes. All towns have crows, for example, which can be befriended with a few regular peanuts or other treats.

Older babies love to gather things, giving acorns to their caregiver, or placing pebbles in buckets or other receptacles. In the natural world there is an abundance of options, from wrinkled plums to shells, stones to apples, sticks to clusters of lichen. It seems there is something deeply human about gathering and collecting.

As babies become toddlers and then older children, they may enjoy collecting special treasure. Setting up a collection area or mini nature museum at home gives your child a space to bring back findings for closer observation. We have a spherical flower vase that doubles up as the 'autumn bowl', which we fill up with conkers, acorns, pine cones

* Daniel Levi and Sara Kocher, 'Virtual Nature: The Future Effects of Information Technology on Our Relationship to Nature', *Environment and Behaviour*, 1 March 1999.

and lichen-splattered twigs. A wooden frame with divided areas houses feathers, dead beetles, shells and stones.

Perhaps there is something even more direct in the pre-language, pre-verbal child, without the words that intimate how to relate to the other being, as associations start to

Evie's seaside museum with objects collected from the beach, including oyster shells and a mermaid's purse

build up. Infants behold a tree, or bee, or dog, simply with their pupils and their brain and body, taking it in in its purest form, reacting with their body and sounds to the life of another. At fifteen months or so, a baby's favourite game might be chasing gulls on a beach. The greatest joy I've witnessed in my children in their first years has been in response to the movement of other animals in the living world, or to a stimulation of the senses. There is little sweeter than the widening eyes of a baby smelling lavender or mint, warmed between a thumb and forefinger.

Lucy and baby Max spending time with yellow beech leaves

Nature is so tactile – there are always things for children to stroke, hold, touch or rub between fingers and smell

Many of us are severed from the land and the earth we live and rely on, for different reasons, but neighbourhood noticing – finding awe in the everyday walk around the block – can bring a sense of identity to place, and can root us in the rest of the living world. It also makes trips and visits elsewhere more exciting, as you notice how nature looks different from that at home.

What if it's pouring with rain? Won't my kid be miserable?
One of my favourite things to do with my children is get outside when it's raining, or just afterwards, for a snail safari in the spring or summer. On a brick wall covered in lichen by the old urban cemetery, banded snails gather after the rain in their hundreds. All the helical patterns on the snail shells are in different shades of colours, from

pale pink to yellow, orange to cream. Evie squeals with delight as more and more reveal themselves to our eyes: tiny baby snails, big ones, a couple huddling together, another moving surprisingly fast. Scout around for a lichen-festooned wall and the chances are it might lead you to some snails. Another great thing about rain? It feels good falling on your tongue, and it makes puddles.

The snails on the nearby walk, which emerge in their hundreds when it rains

If it's pouring with rain and freezing cold, and you don't have a waterproof coat or wellies, you might want to keep it short and judge by the child, depending on the age and how happy they are to be outside. Like many things in life, our relationship to rain can be ambivalent. It's sometimes beautiful and welcome and makes everything glow; but it can also make you cold and uncomfortable. Not every time or day you spend in nature is going to be great. But there is

Hot chocolate can keep a walk going on a cold day!

a strength and resilience that grows in surrendering to the elements, and the unpredictable and uncontrollable nature of the outdoors. Bringing snacks and a flask of hot chocolate can help on a cold and rainy day. We've found that Spanish omelette or frittata can be a good and easy-to-eat hot snack. Spare socks and gloves for exuberant puddle-jumping or exploring can keep a walk or nature play going for longer.

What's the value in letting my kid stare at the bees for a while?

The more we know about the brain, the more we know that the right kind of stimulation in the first few years is crucially important, and that this can be found in abundance in nature. 'It's necessary to be outside for our brains to be stimulated from the flow of sound, light, shapes and colours that nature provides. Especially between the ages of three and six, when the energy flow in the human brain is at its greatest,' wrote David H. Ingvar, the eminent Swedish brain researcher.*

For us adults, one of the leading theories about how nature affects mental health – Attention Restoration Theory – explains why we may benefit from staring at bees. Nature experiences help to restore mental fatigue through a variety of pathways. 'Soft fascination' is one of them: a form of involuntary attention that is effortless and relaxing, often triggered by experiences in nature that are easy to watch, such as leaves moving in a breeze, raindrops falling on a lake or the sun setting. Research suggests that

---

* J. Bogousslavsky, 'In memoriam: David H. Ingvar', *Cerebrovascular Diseases*, 11(1), January 2001, www.karger.com/article/Abstract/47614.

these moments of soft fascination relieve stress and restore central-executive and cognitive function. So watching the bees along with your child might give your mind the rest it needs. Studies have shown that even 'micro-restorative experiences' – such as looking out of a window at a tree, or at the shapes of house plants or onto a green roof – are restorative and enhance health and well-being.

For children in the earliest years, being given the opportunity to observe and commune with other species, and form the natural kinship that all children feel, creates a foundation of respect, reverence and curiosity in the wider world, as well as the sense that they will never be truly alone, but always in communion with other living things.

What if my kid wants to smash snails or destroy flowers?

A note on the unavoidable destructiveness of infants: we advocate a tactile, tangible relationship with the rest of nature. Children naturally want to touch the bark of a tree, or pull seeds off a dandelion clock, or taste soil.

Infants can, of course, be heavy-handed. We suggest encouraging gentleness and caution, but accidents do happen. A butterfly might get picked up with a sweaty, wet hand and then find it harder to fly. Through these experiences, children can learn that not everything is as solid as a human, and to move through their environments with responsibility and respect, to care and look after all living things.

We don't want children to feel they can't touch elements of the natural world (as long as it won't harm another being or themselves). We want children to experience the sweet juicy bursting of blackberries from the side of the road,

Evie making a miniature fairy garden with moss, stones and picked flowers

to feel a butterfly land on their arms, to pick up a beetle and feel its legs walk on their hands, and to stroke the soft raspberry jelly of a sea anemone.

Saying that, it's never too early to think about ways of weaving reciprocity into our relationship with the rest of nature. In the West we are very hierarchical when it comes to other species; we believe we are at the top, and we've applied this to other countries and peoples too, through historical colonising and extractivist mindsets that can lead – and have led – to disrespect and a lack of care. With small actions we can push back against this mentality, if it is something we have inherited, in our local interactions. Stroking instead of picking flowers could be one simple way. Leaving enough blackberries or other wild foods for the birds. Being mindful of not getting too close to a nest filled with young animals. Noticing where we place our feet, and what flowers or plants might be growing, if we are off the beaten track. You might develop, or already have, personal rituals and rites within your family, drawn from your own cultural roots. Cultivating a sense of gratitude and a care ethic for the land, and the elements and beings that we share it with, can coexist with giving children opportunities for a visceral, sensory and tactile engagement with the rest of life.

Sadly, lots of children today believe that nature is 'dirty'. They have been told that they can't touch outdoor elements because they're unfamiliar, and they think they will cause harm. Yes, nettles can lead to tears, but children can easily learn how to spot the ones that sting, and a sting isn't going to last very long. A bramble scratch or insect bite is not the end of the world.

Take soil, for instance. Emerging evidence shows that our gut microbacteria – which influence our mental and physical health – are healthiest when they are diverse. Studies suggest that those people without exposure to microorganisms (through living in urban areas, for example), without access to the outdoors, animals or natural environments, have a lower diversity of gut microbacteria, which might explain the growing prevalence of allergic disorders in urban areas. Scientists have found that *M. vaccae,* a microbacterium in the soil, actually enhances serotonin, the 'happy chemical'.

Children may eat soil – all babies around the world do – and of course some vigilance is required, depending on where you are. But the real danger, it seems to us, is the absence of exposure to these other species (be they microbacteria, trees or other mammals) and the knock-on effect on our physical, mental and emotional health. What's more hazardous is the lack of opportunities for a relationship with the living world that we are part of.

KEN'S IDEAS AND ACTIVITIES

Many of us find comfort and sanity in exploring where we live, enjoying an opportunity to slow down, discover new streets, unexpected places and hidden local gems.

Allowing children the opportunity to explore and share their discoveries is immensely rewarding. With busy roads and the dominance of cars, it can feel unsafe to let your children march ahead of you. I do allow my children to walk ahead, but with boundaries. As we walk, we agree on a 'station': a landmark ahead of us, a lamp post, bollard or post box – anything that is clearly visible and agreed upon by all. They are then free to make their way to it, at their own pace, until the adults catch up and a new landmark is agreed. This creates an atmosphere of trust, allowing our children to take risks, make decisions and find their own discoveries. The added benefit is to your own sanity: being able to relax into the walk, feeling less fearful and cautious, and not being fed up with the sound of your own voice and feeling guilty at saying 'no' all the time.

Working in Tower Hamlets and managing an urban nature reserve since 2002, and raising my family in a small town, has involved a great deal of walking. Walking around the Cemetery Park daily, and taking my children outdoors, entails a great deal of asphalt-stomping. This isn't a chore, though. When on my own, I enjoy this in-between element of my journey: it's fun to employ all your senses, and I like to challenge my own identification skills, peering into the front gardens that I pass. When I'm with my children, I slow us down and point things out, which will be literally anything that catches my eye, and encourage them to look for themselves, too.

I delight in all their finds, whether it be an ant on the pavement or a bird's nest in a bush. We've had many enjoyable urban nature experiences because we've

Creeping thistle in flower. The flowers smell of honey

Ripening wild cherries. They can be available to eat as early as June

taken a moment to examine what we pass. Looking at the 'weeds' in the cracks of pavements and kerbstones has meant that we've seen the exploding seedpods of herb Robert, enjoyed the sweet, honey-like smell of creeping thistle, eaten wild cherries and blackberries, revelled at the moreish green-apple taste of wood sorrel and enjoyed the haphazard leaping of springtails. These numerous, tiny insect-like hexapods can be found almost anywhere, among leaf litter and debris. They have a tail-like appendage and, when disturbed, this appendage is released and they catapult erratically away from danger.

I remember a moment when walking with Amelia and Elsie to Mile End Tube station through a small patch of urban green space. As we came to the end of the path, Amelia stopped dead in her tracks: she had been captivated by the sheer quantity of flowering daisies on show in a small patch of close-mown grass. Earlier that day those same flowers weren't open at the time we passed. I was taken aback by Amelia's reaction and felt so proud of her at that moment because, without my encouragement, she had noticed the daisies and had a personal response to them.

Noticing and enjoying these moments has the ability to create within us a powerful feeling of pride when we've experienced a connection with nature. I love to tell my children that with 7.8 billion people on our planet, we're the only people experiencing that moment with wildlife. When you start to notice, you then begin to wonder. You don't need to know what it is that you see; noticing, for the most part, is simply enough. I remember one instance when we came across several bumblebees dead on the pavement. Bumblebees experience relatively short lives, with a nest lasting two to three months and individual worker bumbles living on average for four weeks. On closer inspection, we noticed a hole between their wings. What created that hole? I was able to tell my two children that some birds, such as robins and great tits, hunt bumblebees and, when they catch them, wipe their sting out on a branch and then consume their insides, focusing on the nutritionally rich wing muscles.

Being able to share the challenges of everyday life for wildlife is very important to me. Wildlife, even if fluffy and cute, is always struggling to survive. Animals and plants are engaged in a battle to feed, drink, survive and mate every moment of every day – things that we human animals are exempt from, for the most part. Our society, culture and medicine have buffered us against natural selection in much of the world. So what other examples of life and death can we share when walking around the block? On one occasion we came across a patch of scattered pigeon feathers. Detective hats on, what could we deduce from this sight: was the pigeon killed? And what plucked its feathers? The feathers we saw had blunt and flat tips, and this told me that the bird had been caught and plucked by a fox. Foxes bite feathers off, whereas a bird of prey like a sparrowhawk will

Amelia and Elsie admiring the caterpillars of the box-tree moth

pull feathers out, leaving their sharp points.

So, what about plants? We once walked past a box-tree hedge in a front garden that was not looking its best. Many of its small, oval-shaped leaves had turned brown. Why was this? Rummaging among the foliage, we came across webbing and, among that, deep down in the bush, we found the caterpillars of the box-tree moth. It is a slightly hairy green caterpillar with black spots and stripes, and the adult flying moth is also attractive, having almost silver wings with a brown border. An introduced species, native to East Asia, it most likely arrived in the UK via imported box (*Buxus*) plants and was first recorded in the UK in 2007.

These experiences happened during the day, but what about the night? Evening wanders can be very exciting. Being able to stay up late and walk among a streetscape that is familiar and different at the same time is captivating. We've enjoyed many night wanders by torchlight. We've seen hedgehogs and foxes on the street, and watched bats emerging from their roost on the side of a house. On holiday in Brockenhurst in the New Forest we went out to see the pigs that would rest up in a ditch at night-time, close to where we were staying. Several evenings that week

I took Amelia and Elsie out to see the pigs, and we'd flash our torch among the trees en route, enjoying the way the light played with the shadows; and every now and then we'd catch the glint of an eye reflecting back our torchlight. Was it a New Forest pony, a deer, a donkey or a cow?

URBAN WILDLIFE TO SPOT OUT AND ABOUT

Pineapple weed

This plant seems to favour cracks in pavements and can endure a great deal of abuse. It has feathery, multiple-branched, camomile-like leaves and its yellowish-green, petal-less, acorn-shaped, daisy-like flowers release a fabulous pineapple aroma when crushed. It can be seen best between May and October.

Those cone-shaped flowers, when crushed, smell just like pineapple

Street trees

These tall, woody structures line our streets, estate green spaces and parks. They evoke wonder and imagination. They create defiance in us when they are threatened. They are an integral part of our community, making our neighbourhoods more attractive and enhancing our sense of well-being, and they also provide shade from the sun and cover from the rain. To wildlife they are green corridors, a home and a food bank. Trees help to cool our towns and cities and provide us with oxygen.

How many different types of leaf shape can you find on the trees in your neighbourhood? If you're up for the task, have a go at identifying what species they are; if not, you could organise your collected leaves by size, smallest to biggest, or by colour, lightest to darkest. Many cities and towns plant trees such as field maples along their streets, and sycamores seemingly pop up all over the place. Their winged seeds are adapted to spin away from the parent tree. Bunches of seeds can be grabbed, separated and thrown high into the air. Watch them as they fall to the ground as helicopters. Can you catch them as they fall?

Brambles

If you've not eaten a blackberry warmed by the sun, then I encourage you to do so. This prickly and tangly plant will find its way anywhere, powerfully scrambling its way up through other plants, creating arches of thorns as it goes, as well as popping out of any crack. In Ireland in the 1930s it was said that before a game of cards, it was considered good luck for the player to crawl through a bramble arch. Bramble arches were also used in folk medicine to cure

Yummy blackberries. I think they taste their very best after they've spent time being warmed by the sun

a number of ailments, such as dysentery, whooping cough, rickets, boils and blackheads, from as early as the eleventh century.

Where I live there is a bramble hedge. I'm unsure whether the original hedge plants contained bramble, and whether the original plants died and then the grounds maintenance staff continued to maintain this as an uninspiring, rectangular block, unaware that the original plants were dead and were now replaced by bramble, or if it was skilfully managed this way on purpose. Either way, every year from July to October we pass it regularly and enjoy the blackberries. Can you gently pick off the largest bramble thorns? If so, you could lick the base and stick them to your nose or forehead and pretend to be a rhino or Triceratops.

Herb Robert

This fascinating member of the geranium family can be found in any little crack. A small, low-growing plant with reddish, hairy stems

Herb Robert in flower

and fern-like leaves with vibrant little pink (or sometimes white) flowers can be seen flowering from May to September. I have seen plants flowering in every month of the year. The seedpods are long, like a bird's beak, and this is how they also get their name of crane's-bill. These pods are like catapults and have evolved to fling the seeds far away from the parent plant. When the seeds are flung, you can hear it happening, and you could be hit by these seeds up to 6 metres away.

Slugs

In cooler temperatures, and in fog and rain, slugs and snails will appear. Slugs evolved from snails and so, over time, they have lost their external shell. In most UK slug species the remnant of their shell is found internally. In addition, when looking closely at slugs, you'll often see a hole – more often than not on their right side. This is used for breathing and leads to a single lung. Slugs are general herbivores, but some also eat carrion, excrement and even hunt other slugs and snails. The mucus that covers a slug is slippery and distasteful, and this is why you'll often see a bird wipe a slug in the grass before eating it.

Amelia and Elsie making a camp for snails at Tower Hamlets Cemetery Park

ACTIVITIES TO CELEBRATE THE WILDLIFE YOU SEE

Dandelion trumpets

We all know about blowing the seeds from the dandelion clock, but did you know you can make a trumpet with the stem? This takes a little practice, but once you've grasped the technique, you'll be able to do this with every dandelion stem. First, have fun with your picked dandelion stem and blow away the seeds, if they're present, or take off the flower. Be sure there are still some flowers left for insects. This beheaded stalk should now look like a straw. It's good to shorten the stem to around 15 cm; this isn't a hard-and-fast rule, but it does mean less effort is needed to get air through the stem. Flatten one end of the stem against your forehead. Then tuck your lips in, place the flat end of the stem gently inside your mouth and blow. It will require some patience and practice to get the stem placed correctly in your mouth, and to get the technique of blowing correct. Once grasped, you will have a nice trumpet sound. A great thing to call your friends to join you in play!

Daisy chains and lamb's tails

For a daisy chain, all you need to do is collect a bunch of daisies with their stalks. Using your thumbnail, make a slit in the stalk of your first daisy, just big enough to pass the stem of another daisy through it. You've now begun to make the chain. Continue threading daisies together until you're satisfied with the length of your chain. To finish it, you need to connect the two ends, so on the stalk of your last daisy make a slit big enough to pass through the flower head of your first daisy. Hey presto: daisy chain, done!

Daisy lamb's tails require a bit more dexterity and patience. Find a daisy with a long stalk, and then collect more daisies and remove their stalks from as close to the base of the flower head as possible. This should reveal a hole. You then repeatedly thread the stalk-less daisy flowers along the daisy stalk. Keep going until you're satisfied you have a nice lamb's tail, or until your eyes have gone funny!

Wild art, Andy Goldsworthy-style

Andy Goldsworthy is a British sculptor who is known for his environmental art using natural materials. I was first introduced to him by name, and was loaned a book of his work many years ago. I was captivated by his creations using fallen leaves. I have replicated his leaf art many

An example of art using natural things found at Tower Hamlets Cemetery Park. Inspiration for the design was taken from the work of Andy Goldsworthy

times since, with children and families. It's a fun activity for groups. Collect leaves of different colours and shades (autumn is of course a great time of year to do this). These leaves can then be arranged in lines, concentric rings or used to outline tree roots, from the lightest-coloured leaves through to the darkest. This would generally mean starting with yellow and working outwards to brown colours.

Berry bouts and wall-barley arrows

Many front gardens have hedges to define their boundaries. *Pyracantha* or firethorn is planted widely as an evergreen ornamental hedge. It's a worthy natural substitute for an artificial fence, and provides cover for birds and nectar for insects when in flower. From late summer through autumn and winter, firethorn can be found covered in clusters of small, red, yellow or orange berries. For a bit of impromptu fun, grab a handful and throw them at each other, as if they're tiny snowballs. The berries are valuable bird food, so always leave some for our feathered friends.

Wall barley can be found almost anywhere, and tufts of this species of grass can be found pushing through cracks and growing in front gardens. Grab those feathery, whiskery seed heads and separate them into individual 'arrows'. Throw them at each other. They stick particularly well to hair and woolly jumpers. In some parts of the UK, people would have races with these seed heads – they would put them inside their sleeves and swing their arms backwards and forwards, which would make the seed climb up their sleeve, and the race was won when it first reached someone's shoulder.

Fairy home seen at Danbury Woods in Essex. We assume it was made by the park managers. We took toys from home to decorate it

Chapter Four

Stories, Myths and Make-Believe

Story is for a human as water is for a fish.
Jonathan Gottschall, *Rorotoko* interview, 15 April 2012

Gentleness, that's the thing spending 1,000 hours in nature can do for children.
Craig Foster, *My Octopus Teacher* (film), 2020

In the early years, before children learn how to recognise a toadstool or a hoverfly, there are ways of engaging them with nature that involve storytelling, adventure and fantasy. At around three or four, a child might become more interested in noticing fungi or beetles or conkers, but before that, a bit of imagination on the adult's part can go a long way towards engaging the imagination of the child.

We've found that bringing in characters, stories and myths can encourage a child in the most basic parts of spending time outdoors: walking in a straight line or, simply, continuing to walk. From the age of around eighteen months to two, when boundaries are being tested and children learn how to say the word 'no', it can be helpful to have a few methods up your sleeve to keep the play, or 'adventure', going.

Each relationship or family will find specific characters or narratives that work for them. Your children might be excited by the idea of looking for the Gruffalo, for example, or a Very Busy Spider, or a Very Hungry Caterpillar, depending on their favourite book or show at home.

There is a symbiotic relationship between the culture that we consume and our connection with the wider world. Even as adults, there may be films or television shows we watched as children that still influence how we think about nature. Growing up in Britain in the early 1990s, I found that the television adaptation of Colin Dann's *The Animals of Farthing Wood* made a marked impression on me. As the chirpy theme-tune rolls, the fields and woodlands are flooded with cement from a giant mixer, and the animals must escape from peril from then on and try to survive. In conversations I've had with conservationists and environmental journalists, the series often crops up as having had a lasting influence.

What's the point of storytelling while out in nature?

When setting out on a nature walk, searching for big, fantastical animals such as dinosaurs, giraffes or wolves (well, wolves may be fantastical in Britain, though not in other European countries) can give walks with a toddler or young child a sense of purpose and direction. Put simply, it can encourage independent movement, for no one wants to be carrying a heavy young child for too long. Alongside searching for frogspawn or butterflies, adding a mythical element can cause the imagination to flare in a different way. A tired toddler who doesn't want to walk any more might be persuaded to manage a few more steps, if there is a chance of seeing an elf's den around the corner.

As the child develops and the world starts to become clearer, and smaller things are more scrutable, looking for 'fairy castles' – the stumps of trees covered in moss, lichen and spiders' webs – might become a favourite activity. (Who knows, you might even get an unexpected phone call from the Queen of the Fairies saying she's left a chocolate egg in a tree root.)

Children love being told stories, and the natural environment is an ideal place to make up stories together. Before a child becomes keen on searching for things evoked by her own individual curiosity, telling stories together can be a wonderful way of bonding and weaving the shared experiences outdoors into something new. It adds a different dimension to that oscillation between the inner and outer worlds of the child, which can happen effortlessly in a wild environment.

All of the senses are alive outside – you can feel the silkiness of a conker, hear the bleeps of a skylark, smell the meadowsweet and taste the blackberries – which makes storytelling easier. At around the age of three, Evie wanted to be told stories whenever we cast out on a walk down a particular tree-lined avenue towards a local river. It became a kind of punctuation point and a comforting routine. You might find that a child will ask for a story at the end of time spent outdoors, or while you're sitting down and having a snack, or at a particular tree stump, or at bedtime, to remember the communal experiences of the day.

Collecting, playing, rubbing, feeling, smelling – the options for engaging with conkers are endless

I'm not really a theatrical type. Are you saying I need to act out stories, too?

Many of us may not feel like natural storytellers. Certainly it can take a while to get into the groove, but it doesn't have to be intricate or prize-winning. A story could be about the troll that lives under the bridge you're about to cross, who dropped his sandwich in the river; or the lost duckling who wants to find its daddy; or the cuckoo inviting the foals to her birthday party. Children don't expect you to be a Netflix showrunner. You could even, from around the age of two or three, take it in turns to say the sentences.

For reluctant storytellers – and it can be tiring to imagine and make stuff up – using props in the natural environment for inspiration (even picking up a stick, for example, to use as a character) can be handy. Perhaps the stick has lost its friend, the dandelion, and doesn't know where to find her. Could she be behind the tree? Or under a log? Or next to the river? Perhaps the acorns can help give directions. Or a friendly conker.

The natural world as a venue is full of opportunities for storytelling, and is rich in symbolism, make-believe and plasticity. A woodland, for example, is bristling with associations with mythical characters, such as fairies, goblins and elves. Sitting by a river and eating lunch can be turned into a teddy bear's picnic with a couple of soft-toy guests. A beach could be visited by gigantic turtles or sea monsters or Viking ships.

Why is storytelling good for children?

Early childhood is a time of unbound imaginary possibilities. Children are capable of spontaneous creativity and

A monster made with Evie on the beach in Cornwall, out of seaweed and found wood

imagination that can be awe-inspiring. After all, William Blake first saw God at the age of four, and angels in a tree on Peckham Rye at the age of eight. With its shadows and shapes, scents and sounds, nature is an arena for the mind to take flight. In nature, the child's inscape – his or her individual spirit – can be truly in a relationship with the outer world.

Indeed, the writer and polymath Edith Cobb studied 300 volumes of autobiographical recollections of childhood by makers and thinkers from diverse cultures and eras, from the sixteenth century to the twentieth. She found that the inventiveness and imagination of nearly all the creative people she studied was rooted in their early experience in nature, as reported in her book *The Ecology of Imagination in Childhood*. 'Uncommon forms of genius which constitute the high point of achievement in human growth potential', she wrote, had their roots in 'the child's perceptual relations with the natural world'.

It is worth delving a little deeper into Cobb's theory, because it helps to explain why natural environments are stimulating for children. She argued that creative mental processes in adulthood arose not simply from learning or accumulating knowledge, but instead from 'the maintaining of a continued plasticity of response of the whole organism to new information and in general to the outer world'. It is through the aliveness of the natural world – which demands reaction and quickening of the mind, where all the senses can be engaged – that this 'plasticity of response' can be allowed full reach. Cobb argued that this wasn't essential just for the creation of a handful of geniuses, such as Beethoven being directly inspired by the little bunting bird to write his Fifth Symphony, but should be recognised as a common human need. It can contribute to psychological and emotional self-sufficiency.

Mary Colwell, the writer and activist who has developed the idea of a Natural History GCSE in the UK, put the deeper, more expansive effect of direct experience with nature astutely. 'If you don't have a rich natural world around you, you're losing the palate with which to choose certain expressions, so you're losing colour and form and behaviour which may then feed into what you want to say and give you new ideas for how you want to express things.'*

There are of course the central elements of storytelling all over the place in the natural world: protagonists, conflict, drama, resolution. Action and interaction and motive, life and birth and death, are everywhere, with all organisms stitched into the others, competing, eating, killing and living mutually.

We've lost lots of traditional, folkloric terms that often have a story within the names. An evocative old word for woodlouse, for example, is cheese-bob, because of the way it rolls itself into a ball. Long-tailed tits have many folk names, but bum towel and hedge mumruffin are probably the ones most fun to say.

When children are older, exploring the etymology of words can make spotting things more fun. The word for dandelion in French is *pissenlit* (piss-on-the-bed) because it was famously a diuretic. The English word derives from the Latin *dens leonis*, 'teeth of the lion', because of the toothy nature of the leaves. You can find out more about names in any good field guide or online encyclopaedia. Online RSPB forums are also troves of old or forgotten bird names.

Similarly, listening to and learning different types of bird song can be made more fun with mnemonics. The yellowhammer song, for example, seems to be saying, 'A

---

* *The Nature of Creativity*, BBC Sounds, 16 September 2018, www.bbc.co.uk/sounds/play/m0000d5m.

little bit of bread and no cheeeeeese', while the mournful wood-pigeon call is often transcribed as 'My toe bleeds, Betty' or 'Take two cows, Taffy'. The white-crowned sparrow found in the US has a phrase that might be familiar: 'I gotta go wee-wee now.'

Species names can conjure up fantastical images and make animals more memorable and fun to think about, draw or search for. The goblin shark, sea lemon, ghost moth or moon jellyfish can fire the imagination. When Evie was three, we found chicken-of-the-woods fungi in the local woods and returned regularly to watch it grow. It was bright yellow and orange, with bulbous spongy-looking fans that resembled hardened lava leaking out of the tree. The fungi grew and grew, like a stack of pancakes on a weekend morning. The name itself gave the adventure a kind of amusing familiarity; and, well, it's just fun to say 'chicken-of-the-wooooods!'

Older children will become more interested in, and capable of grasping, complex interactions and stories. Do you know about the parasitic wasp (*Dinocampus coccinellae*) that turns ladybirds into zombie bodyguards? Nope, it's not something from an animal horror film; it might be happening right now outside your house. The wasp lays its egg inside a ladybird to benefit from its bright-red and black-spot markings, which warn off potential predators. After the wasp egg hatches, the larva chews through the ladybird's internal tissues, before bursting through the abdomen to spin a cocoon between its legs. The ladybird is now a kind of 'bodyguard', standing guard over the cocoon. Still alive, despite everything, it will thrash and twitch its limbs if a predator approaches, perhaps triggered by the

Chicken-of-the-woods is an exciting mushroom to look out for because of its name, colour and quick growth

venom left by the larva. Amazingly, a quarter of ladybirds actually survive this assault. You don't get characters like that in *Peppa Pig*!

How can we make stories come alive, when out and about?
As children grow, so do opportunities for making characters out of materials or finding costumes in nature. A great big lump of dried seaweed hopping with sea lice becomes a

realistic witch's wig. A feather can be tucked into a ponytail. A massive leaf can be an elf's hat. Blackberry juice can be used as face paint and camouflage. It's likely that you'll be surprised by the ideas a child comes up with: they'll be wilder and weirder than anything you can imagine.

From the early years, many children love a safe and mild sense of menace or threat. Running away from 'monsters' can give a child a little boost at the end of a walk and get them over the finish line. And the natural environment provides an ideal arena for creative play. If a group of children wants to play a game that involves some kind of imaginative danger, such as a spy game, then areas where they have places to hide and keep lookout, such as woods or the wilder areas of gardens and parks, will make the experience much more interesting and fun.

Seaweed comes in so many different beautiful colours and can be used in storytelling, or make-believe as a wig

When children are given complex environments to play in, they explore differently. They can imagine being and becoming a horse, and will snuffle and seek in the hedgerows as a horse would do. They can crouch and crawl on all four limbs in the soft leaves of a woodland, smelling the humus and pretending to be a beetle. Even a simple blade of grass can be an instrument, a wand, an ingredient for a potion, a ring or a scarf for a pygmy shrew.

Storytelling can also be useful as a means of passing on values, empathy and a care ethic, in much the same way that humans have always used narratives. You might want to weave in something that's happening in the child's life, such as the arrival of a new sibling or starting at nursery. Stories within the living world can bring moments of understanding about human life experiences, as well as empathy with other species.

But there's loads of death and brutality in nature. What about that?

Of course the natural world is also a place where death – and what we might perceive as brutality – abounds. Spiderlings will eat other spiderlings. The strong will eat the weak. Sometimes a

Witch's butter fungus has a name that can spark the imagination of children (and adults!)

parent will feed the weaker sibling to the other. There is as much death as there is life. This overriding element can teach us all about the facts of life in our comparably death-averse and nature-averse society.

There is value in engaging children with death in the natural world, encouraging them to look at dead things, even to handle them. For one thing, it is intriguing from a naturalist perspective. Second, it can instil the value of the importance of life. By looking at death, we truly know that we probably have only one chance, and the presence of death can communicate a sense of urgency in making the most of it.

You might find that, at three or four, a child begins to ask questions about death and dying. We have found that coming across a dead rabbit in the woods, for example, or a woodlouse that's croaked in the sandpit, might lead to questions later in the day. Like most adults, we don't find the subject of death easy or comfortable, but we've found that a relationship with the natural world – where life and death are laid out as plain as day – can make it easier to talk about, and normalise, without shirking the subject or turning to euphemisms.

Does that mean talking about species extinction and the climate crisis, too? That seems a bit much . . .

One of the most important and, sadly, consequential stories of our age is that of extinction, biodiversity loss and climate crisis. How you talk about this will depend on the age of the child. The maxim of the renowned American environmental educator David Sobel – 'No [environmental] tragedies before fourth grade' (age nine to ten) – might make sense to you. We have found *The Lorax* to be a good story for younger kids for explaining some of the deeper issues underlying the situation we find ourselves in. We'll look at this area in more depth in Chapter Eight.

However, our main objective is to give children opportunities to enjoy nature and fall in love with it, and see its importance and value so that, when they hear more about the climate crisis and nature destruction in later years, they might try and tread lightly on the world and stand against the forces that lead to extinction.

KEN'S IDEAS AND ACTIVITIES

For most children, their interest in nature is ingrained – a born interest that ignites curiosity. I had this innate interest, too, and it never went, with age. Stories are powerful and can feed, inspire and spur it on. I can't think of one particular book that reinforced my interest in nature and the outdoors (apart from all the dinosaur books I had), but I do have a milky memory of a scene from a film that I watched in the mid- to late-1980s, which was a catalyst for driving forward my passion for nature and my desire to protect and share the wonders of the natural world.

In the 1980s we were all worried about the greenhouse effect, loss of the ozone layer and deforestation of the Amazon, and alongside the backdrop of this narrative, a movie called *Greystoke: The Legend of Tarzan, Lord of the Apes* added to my feelings of worry and concern. I only ever watched it once, but there is a scene that seemed horrific, to a pre-teen me. I don't remember the significance or reason for this scene, but there is a point where several apes are laid out on their backs, on dissection tables, with their chest cavities splayed open. The utter waste of life displayed in that scene angered me and solidified my desire to have a career in nature conservation. Initially I wanted to race around the world with Greenpeace, but as I got older, I realised I wasn't that daring or adventurous. I liked people, enjoyed communicating nature to them and found I could do more by helping nature on my doorstep. Acting local and thinking global!

The outdoors provides space to be free and to reimagine these popular videos and themes from our favourite stories. Stories have the power to affect a child's emotional, mental and physical development for the better. So weaving stories of the natural world into our walks and play is important and can create profound moments, and games that last and will be continued by children beyond that day.

In our Forest School sessions I've observed children, over several days, continuing and developing the same game and contributing to its storyline, picking it up each morning right where they left off the day before. They itch with impatience to continue their game, and have absolutely no desire to be part of the daily morning health-and-safety briefing. My eldest says that when she plays imaginatively, she feels red. That is her way of saying that she feels hot and sweaty from running around.

Each child engages differently with the outdoors. When placed in an outdoor setting, some children like to hang out, walk and explore, while others enjoy being active, jumping in puddles, running through streams, making dams and climbing trees. The children in our lives aren't a homogenous mass, so we can expect to see almost every mode of being when they're outdoors.

With Amelia, when she was younger it was like letting a dog off the lead. We'd arrive somewhere and she'd just run and run, and then that run would turn into a gallop and her legs would be joined by her arms, as they became the wings of a Pegasus, eventually joined by her neck, head and voice as she moved them all in unison to become that Pegasus in her mind. This would be followed by neighing and by exploring as she soared! She also tended to flip quickly between Pegasus and a Velociraptor. The Pegasus was a more gentle and exploratory personality, whereas the Velociraptor was more assertive and was employed in new, unfamiliar spaces that we visited.

In Pegasus mode, a regular storyline with Amelia and Elsie is one where I'm a hunter and I want to catch and own these majestic and magical creatures. They have a 'home', where they start and can hide in and not be caught. I am given phrases and sentences to say, and they have to be said exactly or the game stops and I'm reminded what to say again. I have an imaginary truck to search for them, and a pair of imaginary binoculars to hunt for them both. When I catch them, they always escape my grasp (that's the game – I never win), but I am permitted a trophy and so I'm allowed to remove their wings. Thankfully, these wings always grow back immediately. The game continues like this until we stop or we're distracted by something else. The last time we played, a common lizard and a colony of peacock caterpillars on nettles stopped our game.

It's more important than ever to appreciate and understand the wonders of nature. One book I feel is useful to adults is Michael Rosen's *We're Going On a Bear Hunt*. This is a great story about a family using their imagination as they go on a walk in the outdoors. The many schools that use the Cemetery Park where I work have all used this story to excite their children before visiting us, and to help children feel more comfortable in nature. Julia Donaldson's *The Gruffalo* has

Peacock caterpillars feeding on stinging-nettle leaves

also helped, with several Gruffalo trails appearing in open spaces across the UK. On YouTube many children enjoy watching videos of families imagining a danger around them, often referred to as 'hackers' or 'games masters', and in each video they have to complete tasks to discover new clues about the identity and purpose of the hacker. These unreal and unseen dangers can be replicated outdoors in something like a spy or zombie game.

STORIES IN NATURE

Cuckoo pint

This flower tells a tale of enticement and attraction, just like the siblings' gravitation to the witch's gingerbread cottage in *Hansel and Gretel*. Many of the common names of our plants have 'cuckoo' in their name, because the plant is in flower when the cuckoo returns from Africa to the UK to breed, in late April and early May. Flies are the key component required for pollination. The hood-like flower of the cuckoo pint is located close to the ground, and within its centre is a spike-like structure called the spadix. In the early evening the flower releases a fetid smell, which attracts the flies and they find themselves in a floral trap. The

The impressive cuckoo pint, also known as 'lords-and-ladies', emits heat and a foul smell to attract pollinators

smooth-walled chamber at the base of the flower, and the zone of bristles above this chamber, prevent escape and force pollination. The flies are effectively trapped for a day, until the following evening when the bristles recede and enable them to escape, to repeat the process again in another flower. Most people only notice this plant from August onwards, when the bases of hedgerows and woodland margins are awash with green spikes topped with clusters of bright-orange berries.

Rat-tailed maggots

A story of survival in difficult conditions! These maggots are the larval stage of hoverflies, called drone flies – a fly that looks like a honeybee, but cannot sting. An easy way to tell the difference is to count the wings, when at rest. Any bee mimic, like a hoverfly, will only have two wings (one pair), whereas a bee or wasp will always have four wings (two pairs). Found in stagnant water (the dirtier, the better) with low oxygen, these rat-tailed maggots have a long siphon-like tail, up to 5 cm in length, which acts like a snorkel, rising to the water surface to allow the insects to breathe. They leave the water to find a dry place to pupate, and in this wandering stage there can be hundreds of maggots moving across the ground. There's a sycamore tree in the Cemetery Park that has rotted out in the middle and holds a pool of water, referred to as the 'Witches' Cauldron'. It's a great showpiece on a guided walk to delve in with your hand and pull out a handful of rat-tailed maggots!

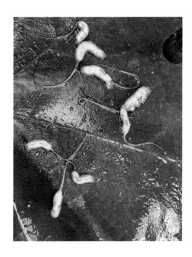

Rat-tailed maggots. You can clearly see their siphon-like tails that allow them to breathe and survive in low-oxygen environments

Plant galls

These fascinating and bizarre structures are abnormal lumps and bump growths on plants. There is a huge variety of galls, and they are caused by a range of different organisms invading the growing tissue of any number of plants. Galls can be seen anywhere that plants grow, on a leaf bud, stem, flower, developing seed, catkin or leaf. Gall-making organisms include wasps, flies, aphids and mites, but they can also be caused by viruses and bacteria. For invertebrates the action of an egg being laid, or the grub

itself, causes the plant to reorganise its cells and create a
home for the grub to feed in and develop, until it reaches
maturity and emerges as a flying adult.

Galls are well worth our attention, as there are so many
different structure types and relationships around them.
Some have stories that seem like something straight out of a
science-fiction novel. Gall-making species find themselves
under siege from other invading species, with some species
lodging alongside the gall grub and others outgrowing and
evicting the landlord. There are parasitoid wasps that lay

Robin's pincushion gall

their eggs into the developing gall grub, and the wasp larva consumes the gall larva from the inside out as it grows and develops. Galls have captured people's wonder, imagination and intrigue for centuries. The Robin's pincushion gall, a moss-like structure, can be found on dog roses and was once thought to be caused by a woodland sprite called Robin Goodfellow. The actual cause is a small gall wasp known as *Diplolepis rosae*. Other gall structures are known as oak apples, spangle galls, knopper galls, lime nails and witches' brooms.

ACTIVITIES TO CELEBRATE THE WILDLIFE YOU SEE

Capture and share a story of your walks with these craft ideas.

Journey sticks

This is a great way to easily create a memento of your walk and try your hand at some simple geography and map-making. It can be done either as an individual or as a group. To start with, all you'll need is a stick and some string or wool for tying. At the beginning of your journey find a stick and, as you walk, collect an item from around you that reminds you of that part of the journey – it could be the berry from a tree, a feather, a twig or a leaf. Tie this item nearest the end you're holding, identifying the start of your journey. Continue gathering and attaching objects as you go, moving up towards the end of the stick. You now have a colourful visual representation of your adventure and a wonderful new habit to adopt. Alternatively, you could use a piece of string to map and imagine the journey of an ant on the ground and create a miniature journey.

Natural crafts – the Green Man, ogres, goblins and orc faces

Clay and mud faces on tree trunks and stumps bring trees to life and echo stories of mythology and folklore. Get creative and sculpt some characters for your own stories. Using mud found on your adventure or some shop-bought clay, head to the nearest tree or stump and make your very own face, or an elf ear, and then decorate it with items from nature that you find, such as stones, berries, sticks and leaves. If you don't want to create a face, make your very own critter that is adapted for the environment you're in.

Ad-lib stories and living books

You could start simply by taking your favourite story outside and reading it under a tree, in a field or on a patch of grass. Reading outside adds a rewarding and enjoyable extra dimension to your stories. Using natural materials that you find, you could then try to re-create the characters and scenes from your favourite stories, or work with others to make a life-size horse, reindeer or person – literally anything you'd like to make – using fallen sticks and leaves that you find around you.

Sometimes something you see may spark a thought, and from that your very own story will emerge and everyone in the group can contribute a sentence or two. All can take part in their very own bit of oral history and storytelling, just as our ancestors did, to remember information and pass down knowledge before writing evolved. There are stories to be found all around us: the journey of a single dandelion seed, for example. Will it get stuck in a spider's web or successfully reach new ground where it can germinate? What about our very own solar system – our sun surrounded by a family of planets, all unique and fascinating, on their own paths around the sun and influencing each other? Or the honeybees and the hive?

An early morning in the mist and frost is an elemental delight

Chapter Five

Metamorphosis and Magic

These are places of initiation, where the
borders between ourselves and other
creatures break down, where the earth gets
under our nails and a sense of place gets
under our skin.

Robert Michael Pyle, *The Thunder Tree*, 1993

It begins with an egg that looks like a *char siu* bun. Perfectly round and plump, its top seems glazed and burnished brown from an oven. Suddenly a dark-coloured creature starts to chew its way out of the top. As it emerges, you see a black head with two neon-pink nubs on its neck, and then the night-sky body of a caterpillar, snuffling and sniffing around the leaf. The end of its body suddenly spurts out of the bun, and at the back are two very long and straight neon-pink appendages. *Whoa!* They look like strawberry laces waving around. The caterpillar extends these tails fully over and above itself, and they're even longer than its entire body. Now it looks like a dog with two long and waggly tails. As the young puss moth caterpillar grows, it becomes even more bonkers-looking. The body turns lime-green and chubby, with eye-like spots dotted along it, and the face develops tropical-pink markings. It looks like a creature from *Alice's Adventures in Wonderland* or a Studio

Ghibli film, not something that lives in the UK. Then the caterpillar begins to methodically strip and gather tiny blankets of bark to create a cocoon where it will hunker down and pupate. The puss moth emerges the following spring, all fluffy and ermine: white with black spots and a yellow smattering across its wings.

This process happens in gardens, woodlands, moorland and scrub on willows and poplars across the British Isles. Thanks to some high-quality filming, you can watch the process online, and you will find the link in the Resources section (see page 211), but it isn't out of the question that you might come across a puss moth caterpillar. This is

The spectacular puss moth caterpillar, seen on a tree in the grounds of Amelia and Elsie's school

exactly what happened to Ken's daughter, Amelia, in the playground while she was at school. Since Ken told me this, finding a puss moth caterpillar has shot to the top of my bucket list of nature finds.

Children love transformation and some of the most magical processes in the living world involve metamorphosis. From their youngest years, games of peekaboo or jack-in-the-box may invoke the first belly laughs. Children are drawn to processes where things emerge and surprise, such as looking under flaps in books or into boxes: those magical *Aha!* moments.

The biological definition of metamorphosis is the process by which the young of insects, frogs and other animals develop into adult form. Most obviously, we all know about caterpillars transforming into butterflies. But transformation is everywhere in the natural world. So, too, are there elements of metamorphosis to look for outdoors, with which you might not be as familiar.

Cocoons, chrysalises and butterfly eggs, for example, are not as easy to spot as moths and butterflies, but they're well worth keeping an eye out for. Have you ever seen butterfly eggs under a microscope? Cabbage white eggs look like tiny, intricate caramel-coloured lanterns. The small copper eggs are pocked like a golf ball and beautifully spherical. The red admiral egg looks like a sweet made from lime jelly, delicately ribbed with white lace marking each section. The common blue's egg looks like frosted icing, whipped by a robot in perfect mathematical pattern. Here is an exhibition to rival Yayoi Kusama's world-famous dotted pumpkins, found in green spaces across the country, at a microscopic level.

How can we see these in the wild?

Eggs are pin-sized and tricky to find. Some butterflies and moths grow clutches, but others lay eggs one by one. Gatekeepers and meadow browns shed their eggs to the wind, laying eggs as they fly, so it's unlikely you'll find these.

But it's always worth checking the underside of the stalks and leaves of certain plants, such as brassicas, nasturtiums, buckthorn, grasses and sheep sorrel. Also, observe the behaviour of a butterfly or moth, and if it's hopping along a plant regularly, it might be dolloping its eggs, so watch where it stops and home in on the plant. Show your children photos of butterfly eggs under a microscope – you will find a link to a mind-bending gallery by leading photographer Martin Oeggerli in the Resources section (see page 224) – so that they can access the full wonder and awe of what you may be looking at.

At the right time of year, it's more likely that you'll come across a caterpillar. Caterpillars often go underground as a defence mechanism, because they're vulnerable when out in the open. Sometimes they are well camouflaged and don't even turn into an adult on their food-plant. (This is another defensive mechanism: outfox predators by going somewhere else.) But there is a huge variety of moth and butterfly caterpillars living among us. To up your chances of seeing them, head to spots they are known to inhabit, or grow a wilder garden with plants that they eat, and keep your eyes intentionally peeled.

We were wandering down a busy road on a summer's afternoon from home to the playground when my eye was caught by bright stripes on a tired-looking ragwort plant emerging from the cracks in the pavement, next to

An abundance of cinnabar moth caterpillars on the side of a busy road

a line of parked cars. Cinnabar moth caterpillars look like mint humbugs – orange with black stripes – and they're conspicuous. It was quite a constituency of caterpillars (or 'army', if you prefer that as a collective noun), with around thirty to forty devouring the plant. We spent some time marvelling at this serendipitous sight and at the abundance of animals.

Chrysalises are beautiful, but tricky to find. They look like leaves or pieces of wood. They're also often underground,

The curled, leaf-like pupa of the brimstone butterfly

so you might come across one in the winter months if you're rooting around in the soil near a tree stump. One of the most beautiful to look out for is the brimstone butterfly chrysalis, which has a kind of girdle that attaches to buckthorn, so it looks exactly like a leaf.

Even if you don't see a caterpillar on a nature walk, or only ever find a chrysalis once every decade, knowing that the living world is full of them garlands our environment with a kind of invisible magic.

How can we actually connect with this idea of metamorphosis outside?

We have found that children love to tune into changes in the natural world. In the local urban cemetery we gave the horse chestnut tree a new name. It is the 'ice-cream tree' because of the white whips of flowers, with pink-and-yellow markings, in spring. Visiting a particular, beloved tree and seeing how it changes through the year can be a delight for children. With this tree, by the summer the early green spiky cases are beginning to form, and by September the earliest conkers are falling. The ice-cream whips, or 'candles', of spring are fun to explore and look at in detail. In autumn collecting conkers for the 'autumn bowl' at home, and looking out for special ones with flat, planed edges, is as fun and meditative for my children as it is for me.

Another easy way of bringing the magic of metamorphoses into a child's life is through the different life cycles of the ladybird. In June and July you might start seeing small black-and-orange bugs that resemble Bowser from *Super Mario*. This is the larval instar (stage) of ladybirds, though it would be hard to guess, as they don't look anything like ladybirds.

If you have a pond in your garden or you visit rivers or lakes, you might be aware of dragonfly or damselfly nymphs. Amazingly, the nymphs or larvae are aquatic insects and live underwater for up to a year. The final moult happens in shallow water, when the nymph redistributes its body fluids and pushes itself out of the larva skin. Over the course of one hour (damselflies) or three hours (dragonflies) the legs and wings harden, and the insect is ready to start to take small flights.

Aren't moths just an ugly and boring version of butterflies?
Moths are sometimes overlooked in the focus on butterflies, but they're well worth getting to know. Well, it would be

Just like their caterpillar stage,
cinnabar moths are bright
and beautiful

difficult to get to know them all, for there are a couple of thousand of species of moth in the UK, compared to fifty-nine species of butterfly. Moths are older in evolutionary terms, and butterflies evolved from them. They do exactly the same job as butterflies – pollinating – and not all moths fly at night.

Moths can be big and bold, with fatter bodies, bigger wings and more feathery antennae than their butterfly cousins. They also have amazing names. Some are descriptive, such as the Jersey tiger, the elephant hawk-moth and the apple leaf skeletoniser. Others are more philosophical, like the suspected moth or the confused. You could make up your own names with your child.

Moth caterpillars are especially spectacular. Some of the most interesting and alien-looking caterpillars you find will actually be moth caterpillars. The drinker or fox moth caterpillar looks like a small, furry teddy bear. The garden tiger moth is literally known as the 'woolly bear' because of its tufty Mohican. Hawk-moth caterpillars have a specific tank-like razzmatazz, with a chunky cigar-like shape. The privet hawk-moth caterpillar looks like a Twister ice-lolly: bright green, with cherry-pink and cream stripes. Essentially many caterpillars look like sweets, which will, we imagine, endear your children to them.

How will plugging into metamorphoses actually enhance our lives?

Take moss, which you can find everywhere. Moss lives in one of two states, depending on water. When moss is dry, at times of little rain, it changes its shape, colour and biochemistry. It winds

An eyed hawk-moth caterpillar that we raised at home to an adult flying moth

down its functions and behaviours and the cells collapse and shrink. It retains its enzymes of cell repair – which the biologist and moss expert Robin Wall Kimmerer calls 'lifeboat enzymes' – in the membrane to restore the moss when it rains again. With water, the moss comes back from the seemingly wrinkled, dry dead, reviving through the raindrops and unfurling, stretching, brightening and filling with vivid green.

It's worth collecting some moss, drying it out at home in any old container and then dropping water onto it, once it's dried, to see the process close up. It goes from desiccated and dull to plump and glowing again. You can find moss in towns and cities as well as forests and woods, so by pointing out the mysteries of moss, you've turned your local neighbourhood into a wonderland. Cemeteries, parks, fountains, stone statues, urban woodlands, roofs, car parks, lawns and pavement cracks are good places to search, but you won't have to look far. In later autumn and winter, when there are fewer leaves or flowers, moss is a sure-fire treasure to seek out on a nature adventure, even if it's just a short walk to a shop or while waiting for a bus.

You can count on the moss: that it will grow and expand with the rain, that its essence, its greenness – its *veriditas* – defines it and remains, even after a lengthy drought. The moss can return with the right, wet conditions. These assurances in nature can be profoundly comforting and hopeful, and introducing them to your children when they're young will give them a foothold for life.

Spending a little time examining moss in the cracks of the pavement outside your door, and feeling how the tiny leaves change according to the weather, turns the street into a place of living kinship, because the child recognises that moss as something she knows – like a favourite soft toy, cartoon character or friend.

The more children get to know the outside world in all its different manifestations, the more it will become familiar and alive. A rainy day, for example, is wonderful spent in the woods, with the pitter-patter of the rain on the leaves, and the water making the leaves look studded with raindrops. A 'dusknic' – a picnic at dusk – in winter brings the possibility of hearing an owl and seeing the moon reflected on water. A freezing cold late-autumn morning covered in mist makes everything appear different, with sunbeams more noticeable and the webs of spiders suddenly visible.

One morning in November, when everyone had got up a little too early, I took my children, then four and one, to see the mist on a small stretch of grass by a car park behind our house. It was about 7.45 a.m. and we were only out there for seven or eight minutes, but they were delighted to see the grass and the fallen sycamore leaves covered in icy frost. We could see the tiny droplets of water suspended in the air. I had forgotten how beautiful mist and frost could be.

Being aware of nature's processes opens multiple paths to meaning. Change, motion and transformation are the signature of the living world and, to an extent, of the human part, too.

There are meaning and life lessons to be gleaned from the flux of the natural world. If children are going through a change in their lives, they may find strength and solace in witnessing metamorphosis in nature. It can be reassuring. It can be galvanising and inspiring, especially in the seasons of spring and autumn. It can also teach us that it is good to rest and hunker down, as the other animals do in the winter.

Of course we humans experience metamorphosis, too. Most markedly in the change from childhood to adulthood, but also throughout our lives: through pregnancy and childbirth, the menopause and the different stages of life. As adults – particularly those who might find change difficult – we can benefit from plugging into this universal process that's happening all around us. Go outside and you can immediately witness the motion and spirit that, as Wordsworth puts it, 'impels / All thinking things, all objects of all thought / And rolls through all things'.* Noticing change and metamorphosis and the dynamism of the

* William Wordsworth, 'Lines Composed a Few Miles above Tintern Abbey, On Revisiting the Banks of the Wye during a Tour. July 13, 1798'.

earth can become ritual acts, in which paying attention is rewarded with magic and intimacy and comfort.

KEN'S IDEAS AND ACTIVITIES

I think it was Anne of Green Gables who captured the joy of seasons when she said, 'I am so glad I live in a world where there are Octobers.'* And Winnie-the-Pooh said, 'It's the first day of autumn! A time of hot chocolatey mornings, and toasty marshmallow evenings, and, best of all, leaping into leaves!'** Living in a temperate climate, I feel so fortunate to have the pleasure and enjoyment provided by all four of our seasons. Autumn certainly has to be my favourite; I love how every leaf, as it changes colour, is like a flower coming into bloom, and that mushrooms appear as if by magic!

There's change everywhere you look – not just in the passage of time and altering of the seasons. It can be in the way clouds move and change across the sky; the sunrise and sunset; the tidal movement of water. Even rain brings change, encouraging the slugs and snails out and, in the wintertime, providing the essential water required by mosses to reproduce. If you look closely (hand-lens or jeweller's loupe required for this), you'll see stalks appearing from the leafy moss. These are the sporophytes and at the end is a capsule that contains the spores. When the weather dries, these capsules will open.

The spring brings a riot of colour provided by flower

----

* L. M. Montgomery, *Anne of Green Gables*, L. C. Page & Co., 1908.
** Carter Crocker and Karl Geurs, *Pooh's Grand Adventure* (film), 1997.

bulbs such as daffodils, crocus and snowdrops, followed by the trees bursting into leaf, the grass growing longer, butterflies appearing and wildflowers on the woodland floor and margins from February to April. By May and June the open meadows and grasslands are filled with wildflowers. In September plants are covered in seeds, nuts and berries, and in October the trees begin to change colour. And if we're lucky enough, we may see snow in the winter and get to build a snowman, or at the very least we'll experience freezing temperatures, so we can break the ice on a puddle or two and see our breath in the air. As a child, my brother and I would pretend that we were steam trains on our walk to school, puffing out our breath, running as we said, 'Whoo, whoo, chugger, chugger!'

As the seasons move, so does the wildlife that we see. Birds come and go, either to overwinter with us or to breed in the summer months. Lambs and calves are born. Butterflies, moths, dragonflies, crane flies, bees and wasps appear and disappear.

STORIES OF CHANGE IN NATURE

Bee-flies

In early spring many photos of these fluffy brown, hovering bee-mimics appear across social media. They're a signal that spring is finally with us – much like seeing a daffodil. They're important pollinators, and the flying adults feed on pollen and nectar. They're best seen on warm, sunny days and they're one of the first flies to appear in spring (from March). We have nine species of bee-fly in the UK.

Bee-fly with its distinctive and protruding, rigid, tube-like proboscis

People wonder what they are and are fascinated by their protruding proboscis, which is used to delve into flowers to feed on nectar. They are completely harmless, unable to sting or bite. They may look like a bee, but they have no organ to allow them to sting, and the protruding proboscis doesn't mean it will suck your blood like a mosquito. Bee-flies are adapted to hover in front of flowers, humming as they go and resembling the sound of a bee. They are distinctly different, though. First, they only have two wings (bees, ants and wasps all have four wings, two pairs) and, unlike bees, bee-flies use their long legs to perch on the edge of the flower when feeding.

Their ecology is fascinating, as they are parasites of bees and wasps. When they are not visiting flowers, look for adults flying low over bare ground searching for the nests of solitary bees and wasps. The entrance to these nests can be hard to see, so let the bee-flies show the way. They're looking for small round holes in the ground and, once identified, the adult female will flick or lay her eggs in the entrance. When the eggs hatch, the larvae of the bee-fly will parasitise the larvae of the bee or wasp.

Ladybirds

Ladybirds go through a complete metamorphosis, meaning that the larval and adult forms are distinctly different from each other – just like the caterpillar that becomes a butterfly. They start life as an egg, which after four to ten days will hatch into a larva, which is an alligator-shaped insect with bristles and spots. They will remain like this for four to six weeks. The larva has an insatiable appetite for aphids (green and black flies). This larval stage of the ladybird is unrecognisable as the juvenile stage of the adult ladybird. After getting all they need to eat, the larvae will attach themselves to a leaf or stem with their hind legs and become pupae. After around fifteen days the pupa will emerge as the colourful beetle we all know and love, and the adult will live for about a year. The colourful structures that cover the body are hardened front wings that protect the wings used for flight. Adult beetles are equally voracious in appetite and love to hunt for and eat aphids.

Ladybirds go through a four-stage lifecycle and complete metamorphosis, from egg to larva to pupa to adult ladybird

Ponds

Without access to freshwater ponds while growing up, I doubt I would be in the career I'm in today. Ponds satisfied all my wildlife needs: they are dynamic and fascinating places, full of wonder and change. I had the opportunity to catch and admire the many different forms of invertebrates that lived in the water, collect newts, throw reed mace at my friends and experience the feeling of being chased by a parading dragonfly as it darted around the pond. There is so much to see and enjoy about ponds. I would often spend all day down at my local pond, and I fell in so often that my parents banned me from going. It didn't work, though, because my friend's mum would happily wash my clothes and let me shower at their home before I returned to my own. In my mind, my mum was completely unaware that I had once again fallen into the pond!

Pond-gazing at Tower Hamlets Cemetery Park. They'll both be looking for newts!

Mayflies

Despite their misleading name, these insects can be seen pretty much all year round. Not just as flying adults, but also in their juvenile form in rivers, lakes and ponds. Swarms of mating male and female adults are a distinctive sign that summer is with us. Their lives as adults are extremely short and fleeting. Immediately after mating the female will fall, spent, onto the water's surface, with her wings spread, where she will then release her eggs into the water to fall to the bottom of the water. The males will fly off to die on nearby land.

ACTIVITIES TO CELEBRATE THE WILDLIFE YOU SEE

Keep tadpoles

Collecting frogspawn in the spring, sometimes as early as February but usually in March, is a great activity. You can watch an animal change dramatically from a swimming tadpole to a hopping frog. The Field Study Council produces a great guide for keeping frog tadpoles. It's not illegal to keep frogs, but there are a few key things to keep in mind. Ideally you should rear them in the same pond water you collected them from; if that's not possible, then tap water is okay, but it's best to let it settle for a day or two. You don't need many tadpoles per litre of water, and it would be good to add a few rocks and plants for the developing froglets to climb on.

Once they've hatched from the spawn, you will need to feed the tadpoles regularly, like pet fish. You can start feeding them on spinach or lettuce, or even rabbit pellet food. As they get bigger you can feed them on fish-food flakes – the same stuff you'd give a goldfish. If you keep

them until they've changed into froglets, then I would suggest that you release them among vegetation close to the pond you collected the spawn from. Please don't put them straight into the water. At this early stage the froglets will continue their development on land.

Frogspawn

Rear caterpillars

Rearing caterpillars to an adult flying butterfly or moth is rewarding and fascinating. The last caterpillar we reared was an eyed hawk-moth. First, and most importantly, you need to be able to confidently identify the caterpillar you plan to rear. It will more often than not be a moth, as there are so many species of moth in the UK. In the Resources section, on page 216, you will find a helpful website about caterpillars.

Once you know what species you have, you'll need a well-ventilated and clean butter or ice-cream tub to keep your caterpillar in. They're best kept indoors away from direct sunlight, and ideally in an unheated room. It will need feeding regularly with fresh, dry vegetation, and providing the correct food-plant is essential. Wet vegetation eaten by the caterpillar could kill it. Lay some kitchen towel in the bottom of the tub to absorb any excess moisture and

The joy of finding worms and watching the amazing way they move their bodies

condensation and change the towel regularly, along with removing any frass (caterpillar poop) and old, dead leaves. This will keep the environment hygienic and prevent mould growing.

This is where it can get a bit tricky: some caterpillars will pupate in the soil; others may spin together the leaves of their food-plant; and some may need a piece of wood or bark to build their cocoon. Knowing the requirements of your own caterpillar at this stage will help to successfully get the caterpillar through to adulthood. Some caterpillars will provide cues that they're ready to pupate: you may see the caterpillar change colour slightly, often getting lighter; and it will frequently wander around its enclosure obsessively, as if looking for something.

Again, what you've got will determine the type of care required next. Some caterpillars will hatch in a couple of weeks, while others may need to be placed somewhere cool and frost-free over the winter until the following year. I would recommend lightly misting the container occasionally over the winter and spring to keep the environment moist and humid. Make sure there are a couple of twigs in your container, so that when the adult emerges it has enough space to inflate and expand its wings. Always release the adult flying moth or butterfly back in the same area where the caterpillar was collected from, and on a day that is above 10° Celsius.

Make a rot box

If you're not too squeamish and would like to experience the process of decomposition, then give this a try. Not only will you get the bones of an animal to marvel at its anatomy (what's not to like about that?), but you'll also get to see the many invertebrates involved in the decomposition process, such as flies, ants, beetles and even woodlice. As long as you're happy to sift through fur and feathers to retrieve the bones, then go ahead.

There are two methods I find pretty easy. The easiest and most ideal method for smaller dead animals, such as a little bird or a mouse, is to use a clean ice-cream tub with holes in it (tops and sides) and to place it out in the open, with the carcass inside it and the lid on. Ensure it is sheltered from the rain, extremes of heat and inquisitive foxes (you don't want to find your box flooded, or stolen by a hungry fox). After several months you'll have the splendid job of separating the bones from the fur or feather remains. Don't forget to wear gloves for this bit. You may also see lots of pupal cases of the invertebrates that ate and decomposed your creature on the inside of the tub, so there's an added bonus there.

The other method is to bury a carcass in a lidless box. This method can take up to a year, but the reward is well worth the time it takes. Place your carcass in an appropriately sized box and bury the box 10–20 cm in the soil, then fill the box with soil and mark the ground with a stick, so that you remember where to dig it up in a year. Once again you'll need to separate the bones from any remains, and soaking the bones for a few days in water with detergent will remove any soil-staining.

Amelia and Elsie making clay faces on a London plane tree at
Forest School

Chapter Six

Into the Woods

To ignite a spark, to fuel a love that lasts a lifetime, kids need to get slimed, scratched, bitten and stung by nature, they need to meet it, feel it. The tickle of a tadpole on the palm can be all it takes.

Chris Packham*

Physically, the creature endowed with a sense of refuge huddles up to itself, takes cover, hides away, lies snug, concealed. If we were to look among the wealth of our vocabulary for verbs that express the dynamics of retreat, we should find images based on animal movements of withdrawal, movements engraved within our muscles.

Gaston Bachelard, French philosopher**

It was an afternoon in early autumn. The skies cleared after lunch, following days of heavy rain, and we headed out to a nearby urban wood that we hadn't visited before. We parked next to an abandoned shopping trolley and red-brick community centre, skipped through muddy, sludgy

* twitter.com/ChrisGPackham/status/984714206527348737.
** Nabhan and Trimble, *The Geography of Childhood*, p. 7.

puddles past a couple of crisp packets, via a small holloway, and entered a new realm.

That's the thing about woods. The physical nature of lots of trees crammed together in one place makes for a 360-degree environment that's completely different from being in a park or playground or garden. Look up: there's green. Look left: green, too. Look down: green, yellow, brown. Immediately it felt as though we were walking through somewhere enchanted. Shafts of sunlight lit up moss-covered stones and carpets running through the woods. The remaining raindrops gave the leaves and bark a sparkle-glow, as if put through a flattering fairy-tale Instagram filter. I felt my shoulders drop and relax.

Look closely and you can find small kingdoms in moss, with different colours and shapes

Of all habitats, woodland is perhaps the one where you can feel most deeply saturated in the living world. One of the greatest aspects of being among trees is the smell. I can work out a few of the strains: pine resin, fungi, petrichor (the smell of the earth after rain), perhaps the smoke of a distant fire. However, there are many aromas that are unknown, but still pleasing. Studies show that phytoncides, the chemicals emitted by trees, are therapeutic, so deep breathing in the woods could have a measurable impact on your health and well-being.

This saturation is because of the richness and diversity of woodlands. Woods can support more invertebrates than any other habitat in the UK. They are home to adders, badgers and cuckoos; dunnocks, eagles and frogs; goshawks, hazel dormice and infinite species of insects such as beetles; and many other invertebrates. Also owls: tawny, barn, little, long-eared. A day is always a good one if there's a chance of seeing or hearing an owl.

Each wood is different, depending on the soil, climate, historical human interactions and geology. And there are many different types, such as ancient woodlands, wet woodlands, broadleaved woodlands, pine forests, urban woods. Humans have always been drawn to the woods, for utility as well as restoration, for hunting and gathering as well as myth-making and community, for hiding from enemies as well as making dens and pretending to be Robin Hood. Humans across the world yearn to be among trees.

Why should I spend time in the woods with my children?
Children need wilder nature for the widest possible range of experiences. The woods offer many more opportunities

for children to listen, see, sniff, touch and taste myriad other beings than the lower diversity of parks and gardens. Studies suggest that wild-nature experiences are linked with pro-environmental behaviour in adulthood. Children will be more likely to conserve and protect ancient woodlands, as adults, if they have experienced the unique tranquillity and awe that come with sitting under a veteran oak in childhood. You have to love a tree to want to save a tree.

The diversity of life in woods – as well as the sheer mix of shapes, objects, loose parts, tall trees, fallen trees, alive trees, dead trees, climbing trees, slopes and ditches, streams, paths and balancing logs – makes for a venue ripe for adventure, movement and discovery. You never quite know what's going to happen when you start out on a walk or a day in the woods.

There is a theory that experiencing the endless variety of life in nature, and the diversity of forms generated by evolution, can be empowering and teach an important part of life to children – namely, that difference is normal, and is everywhere. 'The variety of organisms helps to teach tolerance,' writes Gary Nabhan in *The Geography of Childhood*. 'Understanding difference empowers us to grow and to care.'

The urban wood, that autumn afternoon of our walk, blew away my expectations. We had been searching for the iconic fly agaric mushroom – with its scarlet-red cap peeping out from the bracken, dotted with those creamy, lemony-yellow zits – for a few weeks with no luck. At the time we'd often end up playing a casual points game on walks: 1,000 points if you see a mushroom, 200 points if you spot a squirrel, 400 points for a beetle, and so on. The fly agaric was the Holy Grail, the treasure we had all been seeking. I doubted we would see one in this young urban wood, where the trees were not as tall or broad as those in the older woods that we'd often travel to.

A gasp! Nestled in a wet wooded area, with drapes of moss cladding trees fallen this way and that, were two large fly agaric mushrooms. You could see why they are also called toadstools. It wasn't hard to imagine a toad sitting on them. We spent a while looking at the gills and getting as close as possible. It was a moment of pure ecstasy and magic – not in an Area of Outstanding Beauty or a nature reserve, but in a smallish urban wood.

That day we had all been sedentary at home, watching television, eating too much, lazing around. Tempers were starting to fray, fights breaking out over toys. Afterwards we all had smiles on our faces; and undoubtedly some of that was to do with the simple well-being benefits of moving our bodies. Crouching down to look at a beetle, jumping into puddles, balancing on logs, leaping over stones – the experience for children in the woods is, by definition, kinaesthetic. The environment, if children are comfortable to engage actively in it, requires the body to change shape and move, lunge and roost, crawl and reach.

We know children need a certain amount of physical activity every day. I know mine are much happier if they get that, and then some. But there is something unique to natural environments: they demand a full-body movement experience, which is fantastic for motor skills, development and a sense of fun, achievement, self-esteem, health and well-being, and a good night's sleep.

What if my child gets soaking wet?

Soon after we spotted the fly agaric mushrooms Evie wanted
to jump in a few big puddles. She was wearing wellies and
a tracksuit. We warned her that it wouldn't feel very nice
if her legs got wet, and we wouldn't be able to carry her
all the way home. Puddles were jumped in; wellies were
filled. We sat on a log and wrung out the socks and poured
water out of her boots. It was quite warm, still September,
but of course not very comfortable. In the end, the fun
of jumping and playing with water just about outweighed
the discomfort of walking home. But, as Ken says in his
practical advice at the end of this chapter, certain kinds of
clothing can be useful, and waterproof trousers have made
puddle-jumping more feasible. You can buy waterproof
trousers for less than £10.

Of course getting wet and cold can sometimes be horrible.
One afternoon it had been raining for days, and I wanted
to get us all out for some fresh air. It was still raining quite
hard, with more showers forecast, but I figured that if we
walked to the nearby cemetery we could head back quickly.
The rain picked up when we got there, and even sheltering
underneath a large beech tree couldn't keep us dry. Evie
became increasingly upset by the strength of the shower,
so we called it a day and made a run for home. Like any
relationship, interaction with the natural world will have its
ups and downs. Not all walks will end in smiles, and there
will sometimes be tears and meltdowns. We find it's always
good to have low expectations (or none) and be prepared
to change plans, if need be.

The fly agaric is perhaps the most iconic mushroom, and easy to spot because of its bright scarlet hue

I don't have any forests near me. Does it have to be a grand wood?

I was surprised by how layered and varied the urban wood was where we found those toadstools. Many cities and towns have woodlands that you can explore. And lots of parks, river banks and urban cemeteries have wooded areas, which can provide some of the same magic, joy and delight, especially for the littlest ones.

Looking for puddles can entice a reticent toddler into the woods on a rainy day

At the primary school I went to, there was a small patch of trees and shrubs to the left of the playground, which my friends and I made into a base. We called it Oak Army Barracks and every break time set to work sweeping it, digging and exploring for treasure, and dyeing our imaginary horses different colours. We were always trying to push the boundaries and explore deeper into the wild, wooded part next to the fence. It was a valuable venue through which to create ourselves and allow our imaginations to stretch.

Much of the environmental-education literature talks about the importance of these 'special places' for development and well-being purposes. Oak Army Barracks was definitely this. It was a safe place for us to enjoy and, without adults, we had a sense of freedom and independence. It was unstructured, child-led play, which studies now show is important for improving executive function and decision-making. I vividly remember the comfort and satisfaction of sitting in this enclosed space, picking up and smelling the musk of wood and soil and feeling part of 'our' little wood.

My child wants to climb trees, but I'm nervous. Is it safe?

Around the corner from Oak Army Barracks there was a rope swing hanging off a tree over a dusty, sloping hill. One day, aged nine or ten, I was swinging around and I fell off and hurt my leg quite badly. I still have a scar on my knee, and I can recall the smell and colour of the bright-orange iodine and strange see-through bandage applied to it.

It didn't stop my parents letting me roam around finding trees to climb, and I'm glad of that. Since then, though, there *has* been a growing fear of it, with many parks,

Elsie climbing an oak while Amelia looks at a bug on the tree in our home town

schools and councils in Britain, Australia and the United States banning children from climbing trees.

Over the last few decades a culture of hyper-protection has spread, with parents, schools and local government feeling they need to minimise all risks to keep children safe at all times – especially with liability concerns and the fear of legal impacts. At the same time, the evidence for the importance of risky play such as tree-climbing for children is clear.

Kids learn by being exposed to opportunities to develop their skills and those areas of the brain involved in learning. To learn how to use the body to climb a tree or stairs, or to balance on a log, children actually have to be given the chance to do so. Risky play reaps physical, emotional, social, cognitive and creative benefits. Of course, by definition, there is a risk involved, but a study from the University of Phoenix in Arizona, published in 2017,* found that even though tree-climbing can result in minor injuries, it's a relatively safe activity.

Tree-climbing is a perfect example of risky play, because each branch encapsulates the definition of risk: being faced with a challenge and deciding on a course of action. So are there ways we can facilitate this (especially if our own tree-climbing days are behind us)? I spoke to Ken to get some insight into enabling kids to climb trees, as mine are just starting out. (For younger children, stumps and fallen trees are great 'starter' trees to learn and grow in confidence.)

....

* Carla Gull, Suzanne Levenson Goldstein and Tricia Rosengarten, 'Benefits and risks of tree climbing on child development and resiliency', *International Journal of Early Childhood Environmental Education*, November 2017, naturalstart.org/sites/default/files/journal/6._gull_et_al.pdf.

'You position yourself under the tree, being close by, watching and guiding them, but you want children to have that opportunity to learn themselves and not be told how to climb a tree,' he said. 'They've got to test their hand-hold before they move their feet – that's really important, because if their foot goes on a dead branch, they want to still be holding on with their hand. They want a strong hand-hold before a strong foothold.'

A child might need help to be guided out of a tree, or an encouraging word that their foot isn't as far away as they think it is because, when looking down, everything can look a lot further away than it is. You might feel anxiety, which is natural, but it's important to appear relaxed.

As Ken says, 'When they're climbing trees, my heart is in my mouth, and I have to really swallow those feelings, because I want them to climb a tree. It's about holding in that "no" word, or "watch yourself", or "don't hurt yourself" or "don't do that – you might hurt yourself!" If they don't feel ready or they're nervous, let them be. Don't put them in a tree. Let them climb up themselves, which helps with confidence.'

Wood sorrel is a gorgeous green, and a delicious snack too

It's easy to see, and remember, how climbing a tree can be rewarding, satisfying and give a sense of achievement. The natural world provides many such moments for increased self-esteem, from learning how to read a landscape or spot an animal path, to identifying the shape of wood sorrel, which can be eaten.

My parents never took me to the woods, and the people I hang out with rarely visit. I want to take my children, but don't know how to start.

Lots of fantastic local activities happen in woods. We suggest looking up your local charities, your council and the major national wildlife and nature organisations, such as the Wildlife Trusts, the Woodland Trust, the RSPB and the National Trust (you'll find more details in the Resources section on page 211). These events can be fun and an opportunity to engage in activities with other people and learn from experts.

If your children are new to the woods, asking questions to ground and root them in the surroundings can increase their comfort and familiarity. Start simple. What colour are the leaves? How many colours can you spot? What can you hear?

I turned to Ken again. 'Make it all feel smaller,' he said. 'Woods are such grand things, so you just bring their attention down nearer to them, looking up at something or into something, pointing out what you can see. That often works.'

If your child is neurodiverse, he or she may benefit from this. 'There will be children on the autism spectrum that might create some discomfort,' said Ken. 'A lot of autistic kids tend to enjoy the woodlands; they enjoy the space and the freedom that gives, but you'll have children who feel overwhelmed by the freedom of the thing. So shrinking it all down tends to help, or just going for a walk with them and showing things as they go and making it feel more familiar.'

KEN'S IDEAS AND ACTIVITIES

From the age of eighteen months to eleven years, I grew up in Romford in Essex. I was fortunate to live away from the busy main road, at the end of a quiet cul-de-sac by a small patch of closely mown grass. This was during the 1980s, a time when children were told to play outside and come home for dinner, or be home when the street lights came on. All the children in the area came out to play and, for the most part, we all got on well together: making our own fun, riding bikes, building ramps and go-karts, and once I even attempted to grow a baked-bean tree by 'planting' the contents of a tin of baked bins. My friend and I lifted a small manhole cover and emptied the contents into a water access point. Suffice to say, we never saw the baked-bean tree that we dreamed of.

My introduction to woodland was via my maternal grandparents. They lived in New Ash Green in Kent, and at the far end of the green that their house overlooked was a woodland. I have fond memories of exploring on foot and bicycle, looking for bugs, laughing endlessly, running, climbing and jumping – all while my grandpa watched on nervously, expressing words of caution to my brother and me. When I reflect on my childhood memories in the woods, I get almost a picture-postcard image in my mind of tall trees and dappled light, with endless shades of brown, exciting hills and slopes, and a feeling of awe created by being among such fascinating, towering trees, which seemed at that young age to go on for ever up into the sky.

As an adult, these childhood feelings of woodlands still fill me, and it is something I have wanted to share with the children I work with, as well as my own two children. I am fortunate to have worked for more than twenty years primarily in woodland habitats, both rural and urban. And I spend every October half-term in the New Forest, so my love of the woods certainly hasn't faded with time.

Woodlands instantly capture the imagination, your heart and mind; they're mysterious and fascinating, with an opportunity for almost endless exploration. Little needs to be done to enjoy the woods or to enthuse and excite any visitor. You are instantly cooled down (woodlands are, quite literally, the coolest place to be). Your sight lines are shortened, and you are filled with a sense of feeling lost. You can take it easy, slow down, listen to the birds and the wind blowing in the trees, and walk for what can feel like for ever. There are greens of every shade and leaves of infinite shapes and sizes; insects fly into sun-traps, fungi grow on trees among moss and from the ground. Children naturally, and almost instantaneously, become cross-country athletes, nature explorers and detectives, looking under a log to discover the world-within-a-larger-world and climbing trees.

I can't stress sufficiently the need to dress appropriately, to allow you all to enjoy the woods. Keeping your feet dry is always top of my list. Good trousers or over-trousers allow for splashing in deeper streams and puddles, and also help to prevent any discomfort from nettle stings or bramble scratches. This all aids little ones – and big ones – to get in the thick of it! I like to take a day-pack, with a light rug (I carry a simple fleece rug), some water and a packed lunch. Having a few essentials, to prevent thirst or hunger and allow for a picnic-style comfort break, means there is less pressure to get home. You can wander for hours, take breaks when you need to, and let yourself be guided by the child(ren) you're with; or, as a group, make decisions on where to go next.

Once in the woods, the environment will begin to share its opportunities for exploration and play: a fallen trunk will become a balance beam; puddles and streams are there to be splashed in; the low-hanging branch is a bar to swing and twist around on; and being surrounded by trees means there is every grade of difficulty you'd ever want for practising climbing. All those loose branches can be gathered to make a tepee or A-frame shelter. Remember: please resist the urge to say 'no'! Unless, of course, children are being reckless and are about to do something that is very obviously a danger to themselves.

Make a potion

When playing in the woods, I like to encourage children to lead with their own thoughts for play, with a few suggestions from me at the start of a walk. I keep it simple and ask if they can spot a mushroom, describe the colours they see or ask how many puddles they're going to jump

Preparing a hole in a tree for potion-making

in or trees they'll climb. In most cases I let the day evolve naturally, which makes for a more relaxed and enjoyable day outdoors, without the pressure of expectation.

Occasionally a child or adult will have a spark of imagination in response to something they've seen. This can lead very organically from one thing to another and, in my opinion, these are when the 'magical' things happen.

I remember a time we came across a fallen tree scattered across the ground, weathered and bleached by the sun and, for the most part, rotted away. When my eldest saw it, she thought it reminded her of bones, but more specifically those of a dragon. She began to walk the length of the scattered wood to describe the different parts of the dragon that she saw among the bleached white branches strewn across the ground. Later that same day I picked up a gnarled branch and held it between my legs like a hobby horse, but this old lichen-covered branch reminded me of the scales of a reptile and so, in my mind, this was my dragon and I was its rider. My two children then joined in the fun, both grabbing their own branches and deciding that their steeds made from a fallen branch were alicorns instead. We galloped, trotted and ran and began to talk of magic, spells and potions. They then wanted to make a potion. With their imagination turned up to maximum, the following potion-making activity happened:

- First, we searched for and found a suitable hollow in a tree. A hollowed-out knot on a fallen branch or trunk can become an instant cauldron. It doesn't need to be big; most of ours are smaller than an eggcup or no bigger than a thimble. It really can be anything you find in the woods. We even use bits of fallen bark.
- Next, find your mixing 'spoon' – any old stick will do. It just needs to be sturdy enough to cope with being used like a pestle for crushing and grinding.
- Gather your potion ingredients; this can literally be anything you find around you that is loose on the ground: dirt, leaves, seeds, berries and fruits.
- Add the foraged ingredients to your cauldron and crush, grind and mix. You could even use some water from a water bottle to help things feel more authentic. The water often soaks away, so agree beforehand how much water

should be used. (This doesn't always work; I can think of several occasions when I made my children aware that if we used all our drinking water, there would be nothing left for the rest of the journey. This fell on deaf ears, because they were making a potion and it required water, leaving them thirsty for the rest of the time we were out. They've now learned to save some water for themselves. Experience is a great teacher!)

Once you've tried this, you may find your children stopping at any time to make potions in literally any hollow. We've made ours at the back of bus stops in found bottle-top lids and in the cracks of the pavement.

Create a den
Woodlands also provide endless opportunities for fun and creativity. The exposed roots of a fallen tree can look like the head of a Triceratops or its trunk can be used as the ridge-pole for a den. In every woodland you visit you'll come upon a collection of sticks that have been gathered to make a shelter, den or fort. Most designs tend to be a lean-to tepee or A-frame, suitable at any time of the year, but probably best suited to the autumn. All you need to do is find a clear piece of ground and lots of long,

A den in the woods

straight branches and sticks to gather together into your favourite den shape. The simplest and quickest design is the lean-to – you could have this made in an hour! Once made, have a picnic inside.

I always dismantle a den before departing, as part of the etiquette of leaving a place as you found it.

Build a simple fire

Making a fire, responsibly and with permission of the landowner,* is a great focusing activity and feels very primal. Fires have an instant calming effect on groups, once the initial exciting phase of lighting it has passed. Here I'll discuss one of the simplest techniques.

Petroleum jelly and cotton wool: fabulous raw ingredients for starting a fire

- You'll need a couple of cotton-wool pads or balls, which have been smothered in the cheapest petroleum jelly you can find – it doesn't need to be a well-known brand. I've found the petroleum jelly made by Cotton Tree works really well. Put them in a ziplock bag and make sure that you have a lighter.
- Once out in the woods, you'll need to collect some sticks.

....

* Find out who manages the land, usually by doing a Google search; or maybe an entrance sign or noticeboard will list a contact phone number. Give them a call and chat to the park manager/head ranger. Parks usually also list their by-laws online, so they may state how they feel about open fires.

Materials prepped; the fire is now ready for lighting

If it breaks like a carrot, then it's likely to be dry enough to burn; if it bends like celery and the two halves stay connected, then it's likely to be green and not suitable for starting a fire. You'll need to gather sticks starting from as thin as the end of a pencil, moving up to the thickness of your thumb. A handful in these sizes will do.

- Clear your ground of leaves and debris and lay out your sticks in size order, from thinnest to fattest. Your cotton-wool pads or balls will be your fire starter. The petroleum jelly on them will act as fuel and will burn for some time when lit, until consumed. That's why we gather the materials first: preparation is key to the success of fire-starting.
- Onto your piece of cleared ground, place your cotton-wool pads or balls – you can fluff them out a bit. On top of the cotton, use your thinnest sticks to lay down four

Violà, a fire!

layers of three sticks, each layer at ninety degrees to the previous one, so that you end up creating something like a 3D noughts-and-crosses grid, but with one too many sticks in each layer of the design. I always build a lattice and tepee structure before I light my fire.

- Use your next size of sticks to create the pyramid or tepee design all round the outside of the cotton-wool grid layer, so that the first structure is in the centre of the tepee.
- Light the cotton wool and watch your fire come alive. As the flames reach past the tepee layer you can begin to add more sticks on the outside of those already in place, maintaining the 3D triangle shape and building up the thickness of the sticks as the fire becomes stronger.
- Stay until your fire has burned down and you can spread out the ashes – ensuring first that they have all cooled down enough – either by stomping on them or putting water over them.

Chapter Seven

Food and Foraging

*The great Creator Reason, made the
Earth to be a Common Treasury.*

Gerrard Winstanley, 1 May 1649*

There is a corner of our local cemetery that becomes a pool of wild garlic every year. The leaves are a deep emerald and you can smell the sharp tang as you walk past. One year I took Evie there, with a notion that we'd make a 'woodland pesto'. It was the first time I'd ever foraged since picking blackberries in my childhood, and it was enormous fun to fill a bag with leaves, then whizz them into a pasta sauce when we got home. Now we can recognise wild garlic wherever we go and know that we've got supper sorted, if need be.

Since then we've loved gathering elderflowers to make both a cordial – watching the delicate flowers infuse the golden liquid and fill the house with its aroma – and Turkish delight, which was immensely satisfying, watching the syrup bubble and set. Foraging and roasting chestnuts has seen us through the autumn, and we're working on our fungi identification skills. It's early days and we're starting

* Tony Benn's Introduction to Gerrard Winstanley's *A Common Treasury*, Verso, 2011, www.versobooks.com/blogs/1537-tony-benn-s-introduction-to-gerrard-winstanley-s-a-common-treasury.

simply, but I'm excited about foraging becoming a regular part of family life.

We are living at a time of widespread 'plant blindness'. This term, coined in 1998,* means the inability to see or notice plants in our environment. Partly this is for evolutionary reasons: humans are much more likely to look for movement rather than static objects, as we would have done when watching out for predators, in our history as hunter-gatherers.

But it's also a result of our modern physical and cultural separation from the natural world. We don't need to pick 'wild' food today, because we can find it in any number of supermarkets nearby. The collective knowledge about foraging has been lost, as we have become more divorced from the origins of our food. With councils trying to ban blackberry-picking, and confusing signage suggesting that mushroom-picking is not allowed, it's no wonder people might feel befuddled about what's allowed and what's not. Others perceive the outside world as dirty and mucky, and may be put off eating food from the hedgerow.

There may be another reason, too, that's specific to England. On holiday in Normandy one year, I noticed many people and families foraging for mushrooms and blackberries, and for clams and cockles on the beach. Foraging is much more part of the culture in other countries in Europe. In England the deeper problem is the lack of rights and access to the land. Much of the country is privately owned and inaccessible to most of us, through

* Could you be suffering from 'plant blindness', BBC in association with the Open University, 16 September 2020, www.bbc.co.uk/ideas/videos/could-you-be-suffering-from-plant-blindness/p08rnbd0.

the laws of trespass. We are forbidden from 92 per cent of
the land and 97 per cent of the rivers. It's no wonder that
people feel they can't enjoy the land or spend time on it
freely, and that they might need to seek permission.

It hasn't always been like this. We have lost our historical
sense of the commons – of the land as a place that belongs
to us all, where we are free to enjoy sustainable subsistence.
The Charter of the Forest of 1217 was a piece of legislation
passed around the same time as the Magna Carta, which
has eclipsed it in the history books. But the Charter
structured the way in which people related to the land over
much of the second millennium in England, giving rights
to the commoners to use, enjoy and engage with natural
resources. It enshrined in law the public's rights to gather
nuts, herbs, berries and honey, pick mushrooms and fruit,
catch fish and rabbits and collect wood. Over the centuries,
the rights of access to the commons were diluted and
concentrated in the hands of the few – most famously with
more than 5,000 Enclosure Acts between the seventeenth
and twentieth centuries. The Charter has been forgotten,
and in 1971 it was replaced with the Wild Creatures and
Forest Laws Act, which stripped it of its core meaning:
to give all people the freedom to find food and firewood,
shelter and medicine – to sustain ourselves, in other words,
without resorting to capital and market forces.

However, there has been a growing movement towards,
and renaissance of, foraging for wild food over the last few
years, showing that there is a desire to reconnect with these
ancient ways. Gathering and eating wild food is a pushback
against the epidemic of nature disconnection.

Foraging is a wonderful, fun way of making plants accessible and friendly – and simply a pleasurable part of your own and your child's life – from the earliest of ages. We all need to eat and enjoy eating, and it's satisfying to make something out of food gathered or grown. Also, it's free!

So what's actually allowed?
The Theft Act 1968 states:

> *A person who picks mushrooms growing wild on any land, or who picks flowers, fruit or foliage from a plant growing wild on any land, does not (although not in possession of the land) steal what he picks, unless he does it for reward or for sale or other commercial purpose.*

In brief, we are therefore allowed to enjoy nature's larder, which offers an abundance of options – not just blackberries. It is perfectly legal to enjoy wild food.

It's a good idea to look up what's allowed at the site you're visiting. For example, if you're in a wood owned by the Woodland Trust, there are certain habitats where it's better not to forage, as they might be home to rare and vulnerable species and therefore protected areas. Look out for signs. Ken will go into more detail below about foraging etiquette.

If foraging is new to you, organisations often run walks with wild-foraging experts, and it's fun to meet others and learn from people who know the plants and terrain very well. You'll find some more suggestions in the Resources section on page 211.

Won't foraging make my child sick?

The main thing with foraging is not to eat anything if you don't know what it is.

From a young age, children are drawn to both foraging and gathering, and also to eating vast quantities of berries. My son Max was around fifteen months when he started learning how to look for blackberries, and his happiest times were when we let him go wild in a blackberry bush. He seemed to develop an eagle-eye for blackberries and loved squishing them between his fingers and eating them. As long as we were away from a path or picking them for the kids from high up and away from anywhere a dog might have weed, or from other contamination, we felt the benefits outweighed the risks.

Another easy target are the bright-green leaves of wood sorrel, which has a refreshing appley, zingy taste, and you find them in older woodlands. Again, avoid it near paths, because of dogs.

Picking wild food is a pushback against over-consumerism, too. As awareness grows about the impact of farming

and agriculture on habitats, landscapes and the climate crisis, guilt-free food with a low-carbon footprint and zero food-miles make the hedgerow and forest pantry even more appealing. Foraging can help children to understand the source of

Amelia and Elsie eating sorrel growing amongst the grass. It tastes like green apple

food and the seasonal relationship to what grows in our climate. It might open up ways of thinking about your family's own footprint and impact upon the world.

Don't forget that the fruit or veg bowl at home contains potential moments for engagement with the natural world through the senses. The smooth shininess of an aubergine, the knobbly texture of gourds and fractal broccoli, the bright-pink colour of radish, the soft gloves of the broad bean, the jelly insides of a tomato: these are all nature, too. Mindfully engaging with the fruit and vegetables that you buy or grow, through touch and smell and close noticing, can be pleasurable.

Focusing on the origins of food in your house – that all fruit and vegetables are reliant on pollinators; that bread and pasta are reliant on healthy soil and on the soil-dwellers that children love, such as worms – is a simple way of teaching that everything that sustains us comes from the earth and its interconnected web of life, and not simply the supermarket. If you're lucky, you might even come across a caterpillar. We try and thank all the various elements on our plates – the farmers and growers who've nurtured the food, and the animals who've contributed to any meals – before eating.

KEN'S IDEAS AND ACTIVITIES

So you're out and about looking at plants, searching under rocks and logs, and you may begin to wonder about the plants themselves, and not just what you're seeing under and on them.

Culturally, we seem to be taking more interest now in the origin of our food and the miles it takes to reach our shelves. There is a desire to do home baking, creating sourdough breads, sauerkrauts, pickling and making jams, syrups and preserves. These are great activities and enable us to rekindle the activities that our older relatives performed. They would fill their pantries with pickles and preserved goods. Many of these items would have contained wild ingredients from foraged plants, such as their leaves, berries, fruits and seeds.

Foraging is a great activity for groups, as well as by yourself. It's also beneficial for your well-being, getting you outdoors, walking in green spaces. You'll get to know your outdoor spaces intimately, enjoying the seasons and preparing with excitement and anticipation for each one to arrive, so that you can head out and collect whatever interests you at that time.

Learning to forage requires commitment and time, but there are a number of plants that I frequently talk about, on the foraging tours I lead, that are easy to find and identify. And if you make an identification mistake and pick an incorrect but similar-looking plant instead, it's unlikely to cause you any harm, if you follow the rules below.

However, to commit to foraging will require you to improve your botany ID skills, so that you can take your foraging in all the directions that may interest you. Books and online or in-person training courses that focus on plant identification will help. See the Resources section on page 211.

When you are out foraging, there are a few key rules to keep in mind:

- Never munch on a hunch. My favourite author, Terry Pratchett, wrote in *The Discworld Almanak*: '1: All fungi are edible. 2: Some fungi are only edible once.'
- Always have permission to forage from the landowner/ manager.
- Never take more than you need. Have a recipe or two in mind before you forage.
- Forage from more than one place. You'd like the plants to be there in subsequent years, and there for wildlife, and it's not nice to leave an area picked bare.
- Forage away from footpath edges – because of dog poo and wee.
- In urban areas be sure to wash before you eat, although this is the case for anything you collect from the wild.
- 'Everything in moderation' is key, when it comes to eating wild plants.
- I always say that pregnant and breast-feeding women should avoid eating wild foods.

Below are a few examples of common, easy-to-distinguish, readily identifiable plants that can all be eaten. You can find a multitude of uses and recipes for all these plants with a search of the internet or the help of a wild-food book.

Blackberries

This distinctive, usually black fruit of the rose family comes from bramble plants. The fruit is similar in appearance to the raspberry. These prickly-stemmed plants can form a tangle of almost impenetrable walls of arched stems. The word 'bramble' means impenetrable thicket. The white, and sometimes pale-pink, flowers appear in late spring and are readily visited by many insects, such as bumblebees. The fruits appear in late summer, and it's a popular pastime for many young and old people to collect the berries to be eaten raw or made into pies, jams, jellies, wines and syrups. I remember being told in my youth that 'blackberries are red when they're green' – meaning that they're unripe until they're black. In spring you can also eat the young shoots and leaves, which can be found at the junction of the stems and branches.

Daisies

The 'day's eye' is a flower that opens in the day and closes at night, hence the name 'daisy'. This distinctive, happy flower of lawns and greens can cope with the mower's blades, so it is sometimes considered a weed and referred to as the lawn daisy. It can be collected for many uses; the flowers, leaves and roots are all edible and delicious and can be eaten fresh in a salad, soup or sandwich. The flowers can be used fresh or dried to make a tea, or frosted and sprinkled on cakes as an edible decoration. The flower buds can be preserved in vinegar and used in cooking as an alternative to capers.

The common lawn daisy, easy-peasy wild food

Dandelions

Bright-yellow flowers on hollow stalks, and parachute seeds, make this plant well known. Another plant that is considered a weed by most, the dandelion is actually very important to our pollinators as an early source of nectar and pollen. So please keep dandelions thriving in your lawns, parks and estate greens. They seemingly pop up anywhere. The flowers, leaves and roots are all edible in salads.

Dandelion: found commonly and a great plant to try in many recipes

Stinging nettles

The stinging nettle shouldn't be feared, shied away from or rejected as a wild food. It has many uses: eaten raw, it tastes like a runner bean. To eat it raw, take a leaf from the top of the plant, hold it firmly, fold it up small and pop it in your mouth. It can also be cooked like spinach, used fresh or dried as a tea leaf, and the seeds can be added to breads and cakes. When collecting nettles, it's good to wear gloves and always take the fresh growth from the top of the plant. Take only the

Stinging nettles: many have experienced its annoying sting, but this plant should be top of your list for eating

top six to eight leaves. These will be the tastiest, and if you regularly take from your nettle patches you will encourage fresh new growth and be able to enjoy stinging nettles all year round.

Ribwort plantain

A plant that will grow in any environment, ribwort plantain has narrow, spear-shaped, smooth-edged leaves with parallel veins that resemble the layout of skeletal ribs, and

the leaves form a rosette pattern at the base. The conical flower head can be found on a long, wiry stem. The leaves are edible and taste good in a salad, and the flower head can be eaten raw and tastes surprisingly like a mushroom.

Ribwort plantain: both its leaves and flowers are edible. The cone-shaped flowers taste like mushroom when eaten raw

KEN'S RECIPES

Stinging-nettle soup: serves four

This easy dish will delight all who eat it. I once gave it to all the children at Amelia's third birthday party. I have regularly used a recipe that I came across in Roger Phillips's book *Wild Food*, which was first published in 1983.

1 large onion
1 clove garlic
2 potatoes
olive oil
2 handfuls of nettle tops
1 chicken (or vegetable) stock cube
salt and pepper
150 ml single cream (optional)

- Peel and chop the onion, garlic and potatoes and fry for 3-4 minutes in a large saucepan in a little olive oil.
- Trim away the stems from the nettle tops, ideally while wearing gloves and using scissors, then wash well and add the tops to the saucepan.
- Mix the stock cube with 1 litre of boiling water. Add to the saucepan.
- Boil fairly rapidly for fifteen minutes, until the potatoes are cooked.
- Liquidise using a hand-blender, season with salt and pepper, then stir in the single cream to taste, if you wish.
- Add croutons or eat the soup with your favourite bread.

Stinging-nettle pesto: makes sixteen servings

Many wild plants can be used to make home-made pesto. Traditional wild-food pesto favourites include ramson (wild garlic) and tri-cornered leek. Here we're going to make a pesto from stinging nettles. All you need for this is a food processor or hand-blender.

300g stinging-nettle leaves and stems
70g roasted hazelnuts or pine nuts

80g grated Parmesan or Romano cheese (hard goat's cheese or a hard vegan cheese can also be used)
2 cloves garlic, crushed
1 teaspoon salt (depending on your taste, you can also add ¼ teaspoon chilli flakes and/or ½ teaspoon pepper)
1 tablespoon lemon juice
120 ml extra-virgin olive oil or rapeseed oil

- First, boil your nettle leaves (with their stems, if you want) for about two minutes. Strain into a colander and cool under cold running water.
- Once cooled, squeeze the nettles to remove excess water.
- Place all the remaining ingredients (except the oil) in the food processor with the cooked nettles. Make sure the purée blade is on, then pulse for a few times before turning on the processor. Pour the oil in a slow, steady stream through the feed-hole until the pesto is smooth. If you're using a hand-blender instead, take it steady and don't rush or hold the button down for too long a time.
- Use your pesto to mix through freshly cooked pasta or drizzle it on soups or salads.
- Transfer it to a jar and it should keep for up to a week in the fridge.

Daisy tea: makes one mug
This is super-simple. Fill a mug with boiled water and add several daisy flowers (about two teaspoons-worth), then allow it to steep for several minutes, strain and drink. If it's not quite strong enough in flavour, feel free to add a few more flowers. If you wish, you could also add some of the daisy root and leaves.

Using a fallen tree as a bridge to cross water in the New Forest

Chapter Eight

Adventures with Older Children

This is really why I made my daughters learn to garden – so they would always have a mother to love them, long after I am gone.

Robin Wall Kimmerer, *Braiding Sweetgrass*, 2013

These and other inanimate things she saw and experienced. They were real to her. She knew them. They were the codes and touchstones of the world, capable of translation and possession. She owned the crack that made her stumble; she owned the clumps of dandelions whose white heads, last fall, she had blown away; whose yellow heads, this fall, she peered into. And owning them made her part of the world, and the world a part of her.

Toni Morrison, *The Bluest Eye*, 1970

As children grow, so will their ability to enjoy a diversity of environments and experiences. A late-night badger quest or star-gazing may be less disruptive to a child aged nine, ten or eleven than to an infant in the early years. With higher levels of attention, patience and dexterity, an older child may be more amenable to a puffin-spotting trip, climbing a mountain or picking rosehips to make a syrup.

I spent some time with Year 4 and Year 6 at a local primary school to find out what they love about nature. Almost every child had something to share:

seeing a flock of geese migrating

Autumn leaves

kicking leaves

climbing trees

the variety of nature

listening to birds 'whistle'

fresh air

discovering new birds

watching a river flow

hearing the crunch of leaves beneath your feet

discovering new sounds and smells

creatures

exploring the woods

being with parents

skimming stones

seeing a baby hedgehog

bike rides

catching falling leaves

seeing a full moon

bird-watching

the amount of space and the amount of energy I can use because there's no furniture

picnics

insects

hearing the crunch of leaves beneath your feet

watching the sunrise and the pink sky

the different colours

listening to the rustling of trees

butterflies

As you can see, this isn't all that different from what a younger child, or indeed an adult, will enjoy. But as I heard more from the children, I saw that their interests were more specialist and detailed. One was particularly interested in finding birds; another loved wildflowers.

Our focus in this book has been on an emotional connection with nature, rather than on teaching or facts. But those wonder-filled touchstone moments that your child has had – marvelling at a scarlet velvet mite, or the red breast of a robin, or a crab in a rockpool – can be built on, as children become older and may be hungrier to learn and deepen their knowledge. Their senses are already engaged, their hearts and minds are open to the rest of the living world. As they grow, they can stoke the fire by learning and experimenting. You can nurture their love by providing opportunities and encouragement.

If children are new to nature, they will find something that arouses their emotions in a woodland or by a river or road verge. It's never too late for a child to fall in love with the natural world.

It's often difficult to prise my child outside – there are so many distractions at home and things she wants to do. What can I tempt her with?

Older children are more able to use equipment such as a hand-lens, binoculars or telescope to watch birds or look at the surface of the moon. As their senses develop, your adventures together can take on added dimensions. Listen out for the different strains in the orchestra of nature: a cricket in the long grass, or the plop of a water vole, or the screaming of swifts overheard. Marvel at more complex concepts, such as how water moves from the sea into water vapour, into the clouds, and then becomes rain falling onto their tongue. Or at the scale of the Earth, and the distance that birds, butterflies and moths migrate. A painted lady butterfly is charged with magic if you can imagine the 9,000-mile round trip it makes from Africa to the Arctic Circle.

This will be the case, of course, for both of you. Attuning to the natural world is a process that reveals more as you do it. As you 'get your eye in' and become more receptive, you'll perceive the different silhouettes of birds and their songs. Even if you think you know little and haven't had opportunities to spend much time in the natural world, you already have all that's required to fully perceive and observe the world around us. Our senses have just become dormant in modern life, where we don't need to smell food or danger, or listen out for predators, or find the best trees that would provide safety and refuge.

Your child might grow to be interested in identifying species. If so, a hand-lens and an identification guide will be helpful (you can get both relatively cheaply, and charity shops are often full of wildlife guides). Children may like to engage with species counts that the national charities run each year, such as the Big Butterfly Count or the Big Garden Birdwatch. For both adult and child, it can be rewarding to see a garden bird that simply looked like a 'little brown job' and to know that it is a wren or sparrow or dunnock, because of the different colours, shapes and patterns on its feathers. It can be a great pleasure to learn the names of species. We name the things that we love, after all. Your children might also make up their own names.

Evie calls water boatmen 'water bots', because they look and move like robots.

It is important to give children the opportunity to learn more about wildlife and ecosystems, and monitoring them can be a fun way of doing that. Without citizen science, we would have less information about how global heating and the climate crisis are affecting patterns of migration and behaviour. Older children will have more of an understanding of how systems work and the situation they have been born into, and monitoring is a way of making a positive contribution.

If your older child has come into contact with nature relatively recently, or you're working with children who haven't yet had opportunities to form a relationship with it, find elements that make them more comfortable. If they don't want to get dirty, start off with an activity that will keep them clean, such as looking for bugs or bark-rubbing.

My child is becoming upset about climate change and species extinction. How should I talk to him about it?

Children are experiencing anxiety, worry and fear about climate breakdown, plastic pollution and species extinction. We are in new territory, historically, and it can be tricky to know how to strike a balance between honesty and authenticity and not scaring the living daylights out of your children.

I turned to Lee Wray-Davies, the Eco-Schools Manager in England, who has professional experience in this area. Previously she was a teacher and sustainability manager in a Further Education college for more than sixteen years. Worldwide, the Eco-Schools programme operates in sixty-seven countries, engaging almost twenty million children to take a lead in making their schools more environmentally, nature- and wildlife-friendly via a number of steps and topics. I spoke to Wray-Davies to hear her perspective. She talked about the combination of acknowledging the seriousness of the situation and motivating and empowering children. 'We're very conscious of promoting the good messages and good points. We are actually doing something. There's this whole network of millions of children who are doing things.' From building the biggest bug hotel in the world, to campaigning for solar panels on a school building, from running just one litter pick, to encouraging the school to become paper- and plastic-free, the programme rewards any efforts, big or small. There are lots of Green Flag schools – those with the highest award – in inner-city areas with little access to green space.

Wray-Davies gave an analogy to explain how to discuss the climate emergency with children. 'If there was a bullying issue in the school, we wouldn't go on about how terrible and bad the bullying was, we'd do something about it. It's similar to the climate emergency. It is a bad thing, we need to do something about it, but we speak to our students in the same way. This is what we can do – we talk about those things.'

It's inspiring to hear from her that there are so many children across the UK leading with ideas on how to transition to a different world. While systemic, top-down change is urgently needed, local activism and getting involved in community actions can be a powerful antidote to worry. You'll find a few suggestions in the Resources section on page 211.

At a time when I was feeling paralysed and unmotivated by the news and statistics about the loss of species, melting ice and tipping points, I took my children to a local community tree-planting day organised by the council on a vast common area next to a woodland. It was cold, and we arrived with the baby bundled up warmly in a sling. There were children of all ages, and I remember their verve and enthusiasm for planting the trees. We planted hundreds of trees together, and it banished the paralysis element of my

Cornfield annual wildflower mixture in full bloom

eco-anxiety, and still does. For a child, planting a tree is just as much of a statement as it is for an adult. We have returned to the common to watch those trees flourish, and will continue to look out for more opportunities to plant trees with our community.

Closer to home, you could also make wildflower-seed bombs* or 'bee bombs' and do a bit of guerrilla gardening. You'll need meadow-flower seeds (1 cup), peat-free compost (5 cups) and powdered clay (2–3 cups). Mix them together with water to form ping-pong-sized balls and leave to dry in the sun or by a radiator. Chuck them onto cleared or bare ground and wait to find out what germinates.

Anxiety and fear are a rational response to the state of our planet and the lack of action that our political leaders are taking. But when it veers into paralysis, try and find actions that you can take locally and people you can organise with. There are a number of climate-action groups and transition networks nationwide.

To address the very reason for eco-anxiety, perhaps the single greatest thing you can do, as a parent, is give your child the chance to spend time outdoors in wild or semi-wild places, even in urban environments, throughout childhood. A meaningful engagement and close kinship with a local nature patch will lead to love and the desire to care and protect. It teaches children that the Earth is a magnificent and fantastic home, of great value, and that other species matter.

---

* 'Plant wildflower with seed bombs', The Wildlife Trusts, www.wildlifetrusts.org/actions/how-make-seed-bomb.

My child is interested in gardening, but we don't have a garden. Any tips?

If your child loves growing things and planting, consider applying for an allotment. It is deplorable that there are waiting lists in the UK – everyone should have the right to grow their own food – but you might be lucky enough to rent one quickly. It's a fantastic way of learning from people in the community with extensive knowledge; a physical activity; and a way of giving a child space and independence to get to know the land and work with soil and plants. It also reduces food-miles and you can learn together about growing food sustainably. You'll find a link detailing how to apply in the Resources section, on page 224.

Watching a seed grow on a windowsill can show a child that soothing and comforting aspect of the refrains of nature. You can grow all kinds of delicious herbs, vegetables and flowers on a sunny windowsill. All you need is a bit of soil and a pot – a yoghurt pot or egg box will do – and a seedling, or seeds, which you can even find in your fruit-and-vegetable bowl.

Cut open an apple and show your child the seeds. Plant them in some soil and watch the seedlings grow. Or use a cocktail stick or the tine of a fork to needle out the seeds of a strawberry, dry them off completely and plant in a little soil. You could try this with tomatoes, raspberries, citrus fruits and even avocados. It's a free way of growing stuff at home. For an older child, cool carnivorous plants such as Venus flytraps might pique their interest.

There is a promise and a guarantee wrapped into the cycle of the natural world: that the swifts will return, the trees will burst into leaf, the blossom will appear, the mushrooms will push through the wet humus of the forest floor. Your child will know that even in winter, when everything seems dead and bleak, there is still life to be found, and imagined, in the soil and within the trees.

Can nature really make a difference to a child's life at this point?

The children I interviewed at the primary school spoke clearly and articulately about how spending time in nature affected their lives:

If you've been inside and it's all hot and you're not having a good day, you can go outside into nature and it's a way of getting out of the world and relaxing.

Neha (8)

In lockdown we used to go for walks and I found it always relaxing, the fresh air and all the trees.

Zephan (10)

Sometimes in the morning I feel a bit grumpy, then when I go for a walk to school it makes me feel happy.

Ruth (9)

When I asked them how spending time in nature makes them feel, they answered with a flurry of positive emotions: relaxed, calm, joyful, lucky, curious, peaceful, playful, happy, chilled-out, less stressed, excited, free, positive and relieved.

Children who are vulnerable can reap particular benefits from the natural world. A study from the Cornell College of Human Ecology (2003) found that contact with nature seemed to moderate or dampen psychological stress caused by events such as moving to a new house, fighting with parents, bereavement or bullying. The effect of having trees and plants around the house, and access to nearby nature, seemed to be a protective factor, particularly for the children who were most disadvantaged, and it contributed to resilience.

The characteristics of a relationship with the living world will grow and change, even if there are dormancy periods. Nature is bigger than school or friendships or the family; it is life in the background, which will always be there. The child, and later the adult, feels a sense of belonging, wherever they are.

Iain Green, a wildlife educator who has been working with schools in England and is developing a nature-rich primary pilot curriculum, told me about a moment he'll never forget after one of his Wildlife Wonder days in a primary school. He often works with children who are having a tough time or need encouragement to come out of their shell. He was walking down the stairs with the head teacher when a girl who was in the nature class turned to him and said 'Thank you' in a quiet voice. The head looked surprised and later explained that the girl had experienced a major trauma and hadn't spoken a word for seven weeks. 'We had gone out into a woodland,' Iain remembered. 'Maybe it was just the environment – it makes us feel happy and content, it's good for our mood, it's good for our health.'

The peace and wonder of the living world are for all children. Nature play is often associated with the younger, early years; Forest School, for example, is more common in the earliest years of school, and then wanes as children get older and the pressures of learning and exams grow. We think this is a disaster for children, and that older children and adolescents need a meaningful connection with trees and ladybirds and other wildlife, just as much as younger children.

There is a growing evidence base linking nature exposure with cognitive functioning. Studies suggest that the natural environment – particularly walking in nature – can help reduce symptoms of ADHD, which is most commonly diagnosed in children between the ages of six and twelve. Gardening activities for autistic children have been found to improve language and communication skills and reduce anxiety.

A study by environmental health researchers in Belgium* found that children living in areas with more residential green space had higher IQs. It showed that nearby nature in urban areas is beneficial for children's intellectual and behavioural development. This might be because of lower stress, more opportunities to play or a quieter environment.

---

* Esmée M. Bijnens et al., 'Residential green space and child intelligence and behavior across urban, suburban, and rural areas in Belgium', *PLOS Medicine*, 18 August 2020, journals.plos.org/plosmedicine/article?id=10.1371/journal.pmed.1003213.

What else can I do in nature with older children?

Older children might fall head over heels in love with botany and want to identify everything they can find. Or you might find they have less patience for standing still and long, ambling walks. With older age can come a loosening of the reins and more trust. Older children can be given practical responsibilities, such as lighting fires, or picking mushrooms, or playing on rope swings and climbing trees with less parental supervision. Physical activities might become more appealing, such as swimming in rivers, kayaking, geocaching (finding hidden treasures in containers), kite-flying or climbing.

Of course this might also be the age when you find their enthusiasm for walks wanes, as friends and socialising start to become more important. I found a letter I'd written to a friend when I was about nine. I wrote about a walk that my dad had taken us on in France, which I described as 'soooooo long and soooo boring' [sic]. And I do remember complaining a lot of the way, as my desire for independence and autonomy grew. But I am so grateful for it now. They planted a kind of seed, which I have been able to return to. When I smell a pine tree, or feel warm air on my face on the top of a hill with a panoramic view, or spot an unusual bird, I remember those moments in childhood where that love was first planted. So I will take my children out, whether or not there is moaning.

Don't be put off by a child saying it's boring. The scientific literature from the growing science of boredom suggests that boredom, as a state, can trigger creativity and lead children into finding new paths of interest and stimulation. Giving your older children the chance to stare at clouds, or daydream outdoors, or wander in natural areas can stoke their imagination, enhance their problem-solving skills and give them the opportunity to come up with ideas – just as it can for adults.

'As a parent, you might feel afraid of boredom and worry that you're not stimulating your child enough. But we need to allow them this downtime and encourage them to find inspiring ways to "unbore" themselves,' the psychologist and boredom expert Sandi Mann told the BBC* – and there are plenty of opportunities for this in the infinite variety of the natural world. It will also help children deal with times of boredom. 'If they have the tools to unbore themselves, they'll be able to handle periods of downtime better as they get older,' said Mann.

KEN'S IDEAS AND ACTIVITIES

Many of us enjoy holidays that involve camping, staying in a caravan or renting a holiday home in the countryside. As parents, we take great pleasure watching our kids being kids, having the freedom to run around, play and explore in the outdoors. The 2020 pandemic saw a great demand for UK-based holidays when restrictions allowed travel further afield and the opportunity to holiday somewhere. I hope that some families found a new and deeper appreciation for time spent outdoors.

My family has enjoyed an annual holiday in the New Forest for seven years – we rent the same cottage in

* 'Dealing with bored kids', *Tiny Happy People*, BBC, www.bbc.co.uk/tiny-happy-people/dealing-with-boredom/zdbbsk7.

Brockenhurst, and the Forest is on our doorstep. We spend our time exploring the Forest, visiting places and doing the same things every year. It's like reconnecting with a friend. We'll always discover new places in the Forest, but as my children have got older, a walk doesn't quite satisfy them in the same way it did when they were younger.

Amelia and Elsie are my best friends and my two most favourite people on the planet. I have always had a huge sense of urgency about them growing up; it happens so fast, and I feel pressure from the limited time I have with my children as children. It feels extremely short, and it's as if I have a countdown timer reminding me that every day they're getting older, so I spend as much time with them as I can. I worry that they'll reach a point in their development when being with me may one day feel more like a chore, as the significance of being with friends and finding their own way in the world takes priority. I want them to have an interest in the wider world because it will help them greatly throughout their lives.

They both still enjoy meeting the various animals of the New Forest, and a day there is always spent just meeting the friendly New Forest ponies, Shetlands, pigs, cows and donkeys. We've headed out at night to spend time with a sow and her juvenile piglets in a ditch that was their bedtime spot, and during the day we watched her and her piglets as they pannaged for acorns. I've even enjoyed a sow rubbing herself against my leg to scratch an itch. She was so large I had to really hold my ground to stop her from pushing me over.

Puddle-splashing is always a winner, as are fungus-spotting, tree-climbing and running through water-filled ditches. When we head out for walks, I always make sure I have a few supplies beyond lunch and water, such as a pruning saw, a whittling knife and acrylic paint pens, so that we can decorate and colour in the sticks we find or the objects we make – which tend to be sharpened sticks or wands – as well as the essential basics

Tree sap – sticky like honey, and with a strong scent – can be fun to touch and explore

to make a fire. Having a few practical items contributes to an enjoyable time in the Forest and, for older children, makes your time in the woods more than simply a walk. I also let Amelia and Elsie explore more on their own terms, and allow them greater freedom and slacken the reins, so that they can do what interests them. We once spent more than thirty minutes following the tracks of pigs in the New Forest, after they'd both spotted fresh pig droppings. Unfortunately we were unsuccessful in tracking the pig, but I loved that they had decided on this activity without any guidance or encouragement from me.

Amelia removing the roots of a dead pine tree to get some fatwood for firelighting

A friend of mine once

attended a weekend introduction to bushcraft and learned all about fatwood, which is the resinous remains of a pine tree that has died. When the tree dies, the sap settles in the lower parts of the tree and this resin-soaked wood is great to help you start a fire. During our last trip to the New Forest we told Amelia and Elsie about this, and they helped us dig out these fabulous-smelling, hardened remains of the tree from the ground, and together we used a knife to shave off some of the resinous wood and then to start a small fire. You can find fatwood in the upright stumps

If children start climbing smaller trunks in their earliest years, they will have more confidence when older

of dead pine trees that have been cut down or have fallen over. The darker portions within the stump are what you're looking for, and these can be confirmed by smelling the presence of the fragrant resin.

Being outdoors is satisfying by itself, so don't feel the need always to have a list of suggestions up your sleeve to ensure that older children enjoy their time outdoors. In my experience, older children enjoy being helpful and trusted with a bit more responsibility. Allowing them to carry their own pocket knife, or help decide the picnic spot, is enough. Or letting them decide the route and lead the walk will give them the focus of a task and occupy their minds. Let them get really dirty and allow them to test their bodies by climbing a tree, and be there to provide support and encouragement. I've watched older children design an obstacle course and lead their own bug safaris, as well as make a tree swing. All this was unprompted; they just knew they had the freedom to make such choices.

ACTIVITIES TO CELEBRATE THE WILDLIFE YOU SEE

Night walks

Head out for a night-time walk, with a torch in hand, or join one of the many evening walks and events that happen in the spring and summer months, such as moth nights, star-gazing and bat walks. These are often delivered by local authorities' parks teams, the Friends of groups, country parks, national parks, local nature reserves, national and local charities such as the Wildlife Trusts, the National Trust and Field Studies clubs.

Home-made lanterns, made at a public event at Tower Hamlets Cemetery Park using recycled bottles, tissue paper and a balloon light

How about scattering wrapped sweets somewhere outdoors and getting children to look for them by torch. You can make your very own lantern using a recycled plastic bottle: cut off the top, make two small holes in the side near the top of the cut bottle, thread a length of string through the small holes to make a handle, use PVA glue to decorate it with coloured tissue paper and then drop an LED balloon light inside the bottle. Your very own wild lantern! Or how about simply using a torch and flashing it at the treetops.

Bats and other night-time lovelies

Bats, hedgehogs, foxes, owls, deer and badgers are all part of the night-time environment and can be seen on an evening stroll. Wend your way through the streets or head out into your local park or wild area. Walk quietly, use your ears to listen to the different unique sounds and you'll build up a fascinating picture of what's around you, without even being able to see it. Use your torch to light your path, but avoid shining it directly at what you see – it can be very disorienting to wildlife to find itself lit up all of a sudden. You could always time your walks to coincide with a full moon, to limit the need for a torch and allow the illumination from the moon to light your path.

Bats, in my opinion, are the true stars of the night sky. They're fascinating creatures, super-intelligent, the only flying mammal and adorable. They certainly suffer a reputation problem. When I asked people about bats, as my general interest in wildlife grew, all I was told was, 'I don't know' or I was given misinformation and lies, such as that bats get caught in your hair, give you rabies and suck your blood.

Avoiding the unsociable sunset times of June and July, head outside in the month of May, August or September as the sun begins to set. You don't need to go far – just outside your home will be fine. If you live in a town or village, look up and you may be lucky enough to catch a glimpse of a bat, usually a pipistrelle leaving its roost to begin an evening of hunting for insects. These fast-flying mammals are a joy to watch, and they'll usually spend a bit of time hunting in the vicinity of their roost before heading off to other hunting grounds. There are eighteen bat species in the UK, but only a few are out and about as the sun sets. Many of our species wait until it's truly dark before they leave to hunt. If you are able to buy a bat detector, you can use that to tune into their echolocation so that you can hear bats shouting into the night to catch their prey. Bats generally echolocate beyond the range of human hearing, but young people and women may be able to hear their chirps as they leave their roost and hunt. For some reason, men generally lose the higher range of their hearing as they get older. All UK bats eat insects, so your blood is safe, and they certainly don't turn into vampire bats. There are only three species of vampire bat among more than 1,411 bat species worldwide. Vampire bats are found in Central and South America – so a long way from us in the UK – and they prefer to snack on animals such as cows. So it's not fair to think of bats as vampires. Insects such as mosquitoes are far more likely to feed on human blood.

Bats are the second most-common group of mammals after rodents, but it's worth noting that they're not related to rodents. They are the only mammal to have evolved powered flight, and their wings are adapted forelimbs. Bats most likely evolved from mammals that were adapted for climbing among the tree canopy. Early fossils of bats show they had claws on all five of their fingers, whereas today bats have only one claw on the thumb. Scientists are still unsure, though, as to the origin of flight in bats; the oldest fossil dates back fifty-two million years and looks very similar to the bats of today. Palaeontologist Emily Brown says there is a missing record of ten million years, and that bats generally favoured areas that don't suit fossilisation, such as forested areas, so finding a proto-bat is essential to the understanding of the evolution of bat flight.

Bats are vital members of their ecosystems; in the UK they help to control pests – a single UK pipistrelle bat can consume 3,000 mosquitoes in a single night – and they are an indicator species, meaning that a reduction in bat populations somewhere can indicate an environmental change.

Moon, stars and meteorites

Our towns and cities are lit with artificial lights, so interacting with the night sky can feel inaccessible to many. Some towns and cities do turn street lights off in the early hours of the morning, but heading out then isn't going to be convenient for most families with bedtimes and evening routines. If you can get away from the bright lights of towns and cities, head out on a clear night, get as high as you can, grab a rug, lie on your back and just stare into the sky. As your eyes adjust, you'll see more and more. We've enjoyed many delights through the years.

NASA produces superb information on the comings and goings of celestial objects, and you can track the International Space Station. We've used apps such as Sky Map to understand the bright objects we can see in the sky as the sun is setting. Recently we've been able to see Mars, Jupiter and Saturn. In August 2019, while we were on holiday in Lanzarote, Jupiter was present every evening close to our moon. As we headed out for dinner we would check the early-evening night sky and would marvel at this and be reassured that it could still be seen. We would look at pictures online that had been taken by probes sent into our solar system to study and understand the other planets.

Space blows my mind, and I struggle to comprehend the sheer scale and immensity of it. As a child, I remember a young man who worked for my dad loaning me a telescope and lending me pictures of astronauts, which were official NASA portraits of these explorers, along with some star constellation maps. I must have spoken about my interest at some point and he decided to help. These items were very precious to him, and I was asked to treat them well while I had them in my care. I remember feeling very proud to be trusted with such treasured objects.

As a young teen, my angst was directed at the night sky. I would spend many evenings gazing out of my bedroom window, hoping to catch a glimpse of a meteor or UFO, but every bright moving object in the night sky always turned out to be an aeroplane. Either way, I found the night sky comforting, humbling and relaxing, even though I was overwhelmed by its seemingly unfathomable complexities and how it all made me feel so insignificant.

The fact that I didn't know what constellations I was seeing, and that I couldn't interpret what I could see, didn't stop me gazing. Simply staring at the night sky and enjoying my thoughts was enough. I did wish, though, that I had a section of roof I could climb out onto and lie down on, like in the movies. Lying down is definitely the best way to star-gaze!

Rockpools and crabbing

These are two of our most favourite activities and they're timeless. I have many fond memories of rockpooling as a child, and as part of studying for my degree in environmental biology. Britain has thousands of miles of coastline, so you have a lot of choice, but do follow all the coastal warnings. Each rockpool can feel like opening a new present. There's something different to see and discover in every pool.

Approach gently and quietly, then crouch at the edge to get yourself out of view of the pool's residents. With patience, the rockpool's residents will begin to show themselves – you can entice them out with the same food you would use to catch crabs (see below). Using a swimming mask

A seaweed playpen!

will help you see into the pool better. Just push the mask gently into the water surface: *voilà*, you have a window into this fascinating world. Anything you move in the rockpool, such as rocks and stones, should always be placed back where they were found, as far as possible, after you've had a look underneath.

I spent many summers as a teenager down by the River Crouch, a river that flows entirely through the county of Essex into the English Channel. The section I used to crab in is tidal seawater and was always a great spot for catching crabs, eels and small fish, as well as for running through the mudflats, saying out loud, 'I'm as light a feather', believing that this made me lighter and less likely to get stuck or to lose a shoe in the mud.

At work we once had a group of volunteers with us, and one of the volunteers was from Italy. He told me, when we were weeding out stinging nettles, that he and his friends used to run through nettle patches saying, 'I won't get stung', believing that this made them impervious to nettle stings. He said it worked. Nettles work by being brushed against gently, so maybe this chap and his friends consistently ran so fast that the nettles weren't able to sting them. But I digress – sorry!

Back to crabbing: very little is needed to catch and enjoy crabs. First, once again adhere to any coastal warnings. It's best to crab as the tide is high or coming in, and certainly before it starts to go out. Crabs are smart and so, when the tide turns to go out, they begin to move into deeper water to avoid getting caught out in the open, thereby limiting the likelihood of a catch. You will require some kind of fishing line, with a net bag to hold your bait. Sardines and fish heads are best. At a pinch, though, smokeless bacon and ham will work well; or some potted fishpaste. Finally, a bucket with some water (taken from your fishing spot) to hold your caught crabs. Don't keep them in there too long, especially on a hot day, as the fresh water will evaporate and make the rest unpleasantly saline for your bucket inhabitants.

Crabbing: an activity every child (and adult) should do

Chapter Nine

Rewilding Childhood

There was a child went forth every day,
And the first object he looked upon,
that object he became,
And that object became part of him for
the day or a certain part of the day,
Or for many years or stretching
cycles of years.

Walt Whitman, 'There was a Child Went Forth', *Leaves of Grass*, 1855

As the evidence mounts about the importance of nature for health and well-being, and our time outdoors diminishes as nature is depleted, two things are crystal-clear: people need nature, and our society's relationship to the living world needs an upgrade.

When I visited the primary-school children, I asked both classes if they wanted to spend more time in nature or less. In Year 4, 95 per cent wanted more time. In Year 6, it was around 80 per cent. In 2011 Unicef asked children what they needed to be happy, and the top three answers were: time, friendships and the outdoors. We need to start seeing time in nature as just as important as eating fruit and vegetables or getting a good night's sleep.

Teachers, parents and educators *want* children to spend more time in nature. There is enthusiasm and a deep sense

Spending time in the woods is beneficial for everyone's mental and physical health

that it isn't good for children to be cooped up, as they are in our modern world, but for various reasons it seems out of reach. So, having talked to adults and read various books, I decided to go directly to the children and find out how they would solve the problem. If you were mayor of this town for one day, I asked the two year-groups, how would you give children more time in the natural world? What would you change?

Their answers were fascinating. Some were wonderfully radical, while others matched what adults had told me about the barriers between children and nature. Even the most far-out ideas had a core of clear-eyed wisdom to them. For example, one Year 6 boy suggested having no doors on buildings, so that animals could come freely in and out, which made everyone chuckle; but it wasn't that long ago that there were hundreds of open-air schools across Britain and Europe, in which children learned in big rooms without walls to reap the benefits of fresh air, at a time of TB and other diseases.

What, then, did our cohort suggest?

everyone has a garden

extra playtime outside

everyone has to spend fifteen minutes outside in the morning

plant more trees

more play outside

stop litter

everyone has a dog to take out

everyone has to plant one tree or bush and water it and look after it

more time outside

more nature

fewer lessons

less air pollution

a safe place to play without parents where animals and kids can go

More parks

protect endangered species

stop cutting down trees

looking for wildlife at school

less homework

more classes outside

less driving and more walking

an annual nature day where everybody goes out

We live in a society where nature is put in a box to one side. Grass in public areas is mown to within an inch of its life, wildlife is vilified, ancient trees are destroyed, children's playgrounds are lifeless, property developers net trees to stop birds nesting or feeding. We like nature, as long as it's on our terms. Everywhere you look, nature is a footnote, an extra. We don't, as a society, believe – judging by our actions – that nature is important in and of itself, or that opportunities to spend time in nature are of the highest value and significance.

This attitude does us all a disservice, not only the wild species and places that are destroyed as this mentality reigns. Children especially, for all the reasons we have explored, require a meaningful connection with the rest of nature in their everyday lives – not just as an occasional add-on.

Of course centuries of history and culture have led to this point, where we perceive 'nature' as something apart from us, something to be used or visited, and there is no going back to the time before the Industrial Revolution. We live in a society built around production, and along with the rise of social media and technology, there are many shiny things designed to draw our attention and time away from the everyday world. Children are trapped indoors because of the way that our urban and rural areas have been built to accommodate the dominance of cars and other motor vehicles. But we can work towards a more nature-friendly, wildlife-friendly, beautiful world and shed the exploitation and domination that have defined our relationship with our wider environment in recent history. We can tune into exactly what we have already lost and

The freedom of the forest

what we are losing, and make our feelings known. But we need top-down structural and political change. Inspired by the primary-school children's vision, and influenced by their suggestions, here are some ideas for children and nature reform.

Housing, planning and urban design

The way our towns and cities are designed has exaggerated our disconnection from the natural world. Both children and nature are neglected and disregarded in housing plans and urban design. Can we build housing developments that include the needs and desires of children for wild play? The odd swing or slide in a housing estate is not good enough. What if trees and vegetation were built into estate plans, not just for health and flood relief and carbon capture, but also for awe, wonder and beauty? What about more green roofs across urban areas? Or ponds and drainage systems that imitate nature and provide habitats for our declining wildlife? Or wildlife crossings built into busy roads to link up fragmented habitats?

Roadside nature reserves, verges buzzing with insects, amenity space filled with trees, roundabouts covered in wildflowers, bird boxes on every new development in England, swift boxes built into housing plans, less mowing . . . There are so many ways that nature could thrive in our urban and rural neighbourhoods, if we can get over our obsession with neatness.

Relaxing the management of green space will create diverse and dynamic environments for children, as well as enhance biodiversity and bring life, colour and beauty to people's lives. It's a powerful, low-maintenance fix that would save money, too.

People often complain to councils that 'wilder' areas or urban meadows can look messy and untidy. Shouldn't Defra (the Department for Environment, Food and Rural Affairs) invest in a public information campaign about the importance of invertebrates and the biodiversity crisis? No one truly wants to live in a nature-unfriendly landscape.

What can we do now? Write to our MPs and councillors and say we want more nature. Plant a tree with a community group. Mow a patch of our own lawns less.

Playgrounds

Why do we put up with sterile, prescriptive playgrounds, without the trees, loose parts and greenery necessary for children to be physically active, interact joyfully and imaginatively with their surroundings, and explore and discover?

Our local playground has the standard swings, slide, climbing frame and roundabout, and my children are bored after about forty minutes. There is only one thing a child can do on a swing or slide. For an adult, pushing a swing for half an hour has to be up there among the most mind-numbingly boring activities of all time. Children need trees to take shade under on hot days, and leaves to play with; wild play areas they can nest in; open space through which they can run as fast as possible; and a combination of special places and natural materials. A tree trunk can become the tale of an ancient monster, a castle, a restaurant, a snake. With the absence of other species, children are losing characters in their stories and imagination, and the sense that they are part of a wider matrix of beings.

Parks

Considering the now-proven health benefits of nature, it is wrong-headed and damaging that park budgets are often slashed. Park funding for the health and well-being of people and other animals should be ring-fenced. Wilder areas that support greater biodiversity and play opportunities should be a priority. Parks and green spaces could also be better designed with the needs and preferences of local communities in mind, combining the requirement for species habitats with aesthetic preferences that support well-being.

Creating safer routes to parks, and connecting green space through green corridors (or, as it is called in Tower Hamlets, the Green Grid network), will make it more appealing for people to access natural spaces. If children could get to parks and woods without crossing roads, would we allow them more freedom to explore the rest of the living world with their friends and spend time there without us?

Schools and the curriculum

'Every teacher that I've ever met would love to have freedom,' said Manu Maunganidze, founder of Nature Youth Connections and Education (NYCE) and a teacher for many years. 'Freedom to go outside when they see fit.' What if teachers could take lessons outside – not just science or geography, but music and maths, too?

'Kids learn more when they find what they're doing relevant, or fun, or connective,' said Maunganidze.

For younger children, the tangible – what they can touch and feel and see – is important. He has spent years weaving nature into his lesson plans.

'I was lucky that I was at a school where I was allowed to think quite openly about what it means to learn your times tables. Is there an opportunity to go outside and count the number of leaves on a twig and imagine if there are a hundred twigs on that tree, how many leaves are there? Is it exponentially more beneficial to walk around a field and actually imagine and see what an acre, a hectare actually is, and picture how much grass a cow is going to eat this year, and then write about that when you get back to the classroom?'

For schools to incorporate nature and the outdoors more fully into the everyday lives of children, the Department of Education's method of measuring attainment and progress would need to evolve, says Maunganidze.

'We have a society that loves to measure everything, loves everything in a nice tick-box form: this person is doing well, that person has met their target. You can't measure kids going out and learning through nature. It just doesn't make sense.

Enjoying the sound of the woods in the rain

The measurement would have to be totally different and the people doing the measuring would have to be totally retrained.'

There are many inspiring organisations calling for change, including initiatives such as Outdoor Classroom Day; Nature Premium, which gives funding to schools that have less green space; the OPAL Primary Programme, which creates better play spaces for schools; and the Nature Friendly Schools programme led by the Wildlife Trusts.

But shouldn't all schools be nature-friendly? Shouldn't all new developments include outdoor classrooms in their plans? Could the Department of Education invest in proper outdoor waterproof clothes, so that all children can go outside and play every day, whatever the weather? Where is the government inquiry into outdoor learning?

Forest School is a groundbreaking movement in the UK that's been growing for decades. We would wish every school in the country to have a trained Forest School leader, so that all children can experience building a fire, taking risks, tool use and the outdoors. But with the stress of the curriculum, pressure to deliver and the lack of time, it is difficult for teachers to train and to take children outside, unless they have strong, empowering leadership and parents who are happy for children to come home a bit muddy.

Again, this points to the need for structural societal change. Letting children be children. Prioritising learning through engagement and the senses. Instilling an interest in the wider world via direct, active experience. Tackling the epidemic of ecological illiteracy. Allowing children to listen and talk to the natural world, without quashing their innate love and interest.

Cars, roads and safety

The creeping dominance of motorised vehicles is a huge factor in modern nature deprivation. Children can't play outside their front doors, because it's not safe, which is an oft-overlooked reason for nature deprivation. Playing Out – a Bristol-based organisation that started the now-international resident-led 'play streets' movement – has been campaigning for years about this, recognising that while children need access to the big, beautiful parks and forests, they also need to be able to go literally outside their front door and experience play right there.

'It's become that roads are for cars – that's the culture now – but actually roads were built before cars existed. Gradually, gradually, people have been pushed to the side and pushed indoors,' said Ingrid Skeels, a director at Playing Out.

Even if children live near a beautiful green space with lots of play opportunities, if they have to cross many roads to get there, it's never going to be a daily option. The Playing Out group sees the prevalence of digital screens as a symptom, rather than the cause, of eco-alienation.

'People talk about screens being the reason why children are in,' said Skeels. 'Obviously it's a massive lure for good and for bad. But when we do play-streets, children do tend to come out. They still want that.' She went on, 'Children are trapped inside; they've had to become more indoors and find things to do. It would be interesting if the digital revolution hadn't happened, but car ownership had gone up – I think people would have revolted by now. We would all have been trapped inside with children, with nothing to do.'

Car-free days, and designing and changing towns and cities so that people can get around without cars, is an urgent priority, which would result in the improved health and well-being of people. It seems strange that we've lost sight of the dangers of our car-filled world, and have acquiesced to their dominance.

But without acknowledgement at the top of politics, and a cultural shift in understanding about what children need, said Skeels, every change is going to be a massive battle.

'If there was an acknowledgement that children fundamentally need to play out with other children, for their well-being, mental and physical health, resilience and independence, and that's also a right – there is a "right to play" in the UN Convention on the Rights of the Child – that would filter down into different areas. Transport would have to think about slowing down residential roads because we've said this. Housing would say, "Hang on, we're designing new social housing, obviously we've got to design space for this important thing that we've all said children must do."'

She points to a strangely obvious blind spot in public health policy and tackling obesity: making environments safer to play in, because that's where children will naturally be active and get their 'exercise'. 'This is a major shift that has to happen if we want our children to grow up healthy and happy, with a sense of belonging to their patch.'

In Wales, children's rights to play are protected by law. Local authorities must assess and secure 'sufficient play opportunities for children in their areas'. Why isn't this the case in the other nations of the United Kingdom?

Land injustice, racism and inequality of access

We have a problem in England with inequality of access to nature. Part of the issue is that we are cut off from the vast majority of land because of the laws of trespass. An extended Right to Roam – similar to that in Scotland and other European countries – would make it easier for people to wander, ramble, swim, kayak, forage and climb, and build a responsible and kind relationship with our wild landscapes. But what about the increase in littering and trashing of natural spaces that was reported during the lockdown of 2020? The government has spent less than

Opportunities for taking risks in woodlands are manifold

£2,000 a year on promoting the Countryside Code since 2010. Our money could be spent doing more to foster a nurturing and respectful relationship with nature. Talking about the Code at home with children, as well as in schools, would help.

A lack of representation of people of colour in the nature sectors in the UK, as well as the hostility and exclusion experienced by black and other minority ethnic groups in natural environments, prevents all people enjoying the benefits that the outdoor world has to offer. Because our society believes that nature is a luxury element, rather than part of an everyday need, the people who necessarily work in the nature-connection world are usually from a certain socioeconomic and demographic background, says Manu Maunganidze. More diverse representation would help close the gap in understanding and, therefore, in access.

While working at a private school for seven years he met children who were more likely to, for example, visit an arboretum on a weekend after learning about leaves that week at school. When he moved to teaching at a state-funded school, he realised the inequality of access to nature. 'That's so much less likely to happen for a child who doesn't have that cultural and economic capital,' he said.

For further insight, Ken spoke to his colleague and friend Dimuthu Meehitiya, the education manager at the Soanes Centre for Setpoint London East. Dim delivers environmental education in the Cemetery Park, and his family is of Sri Lankan heritage. Ken asked Dim about his experience of working in the natural world and the barriers and obstacles he has seen for people of colour (POC) accessing nature and the countryside:

I'm surprised when I see people of colour in nature reserves. Being a person of colour myself, we do greet each other, say hi – stuff like that. But in more recent years I've definitely seen people from different communities using green space a lot more. I see more Black and Asian people visiting towns like

Lyme Regis, for example, where I've been going for fifteen years. When I started working in nature conservation in the nineties, though, nature reserves or woodland walks were seen as quite upper-class relaxation spots, whilst people like us would go to green desert-style parks to have BBQs and play football and cricket.

One problem is that people of colour, or those from low-income backgrounds, don't really feel like the countryside and nature have been opened up to them. Certain things are opened up to POC, in terms of recreation, but going to a woodland, for example, just for a walk: there are access issues. You need to have the right shoes and clothing, and a lot of people don't have those things. It can be quite expensive to feel comfortable in the woods.

Also, there may be a physical difficulty for POC or low-income families actually getting to nature reserves and the countryside, if they don't own a car. Public transport access is a big issue in the countryside. That's why nature reserves in urban areas like Tower Hamlets Cemetery Park are really important.

Another issue is not feeling welcome. People say, 'Everyone is friendly in the countryside', but that's not always been my perception of it. People can be friendly, but it depends who you're with. If I'm with white people, it tends to be slightly different. If I'm with a load of boys who are brown, if we're outnumbering, you get the feeling of people thinking, 'There goes the neighbourhood.' Your first perception is: I'm feeling a bit scared – are we welcome?

Why aren't there more people of colour in nature jobs? If you're from an aspirational immigrant family, your parents' idea of a good job would be doctor or lawyer. Back in the day, the only real understanding of conservation degrees was marine biology, and the only people that did that were kids that were taken skiing, or to Tanzania to take photographs. It was never a course I thought of doing. The courses weren't really in the spectrum for me. My dad had been pushing me to be an engineer, but somehow he'd found this course: environmental management.

Because I know what I'm doing and I can talk well, I've had positive opportunities where organisations employed me, often with excitement. I've been in every publication – get Dim out for the photographs! But I've always been a minority in the organisations. Representation is important. When I got into the nature-conservation world, there weren't any people who were Black or Asian.

Once they realised that I had my own mind and I wasn't going to fit the mould, my experiences became negative. My voice was quelled. In a twenty-year career, I've only had two jobs where I was allowed to be me. Whenever I've brought things up – and with the BLM movement there's a language now, for unconscious bias, code-talking, and so on – I wasn't taken seriously. People assume you got your job through affirmative action, and a lot of people have done that to me.

After knowing me for a year, and observing my lessons, a senior employee at an established museum said, 'You're actually very good at your job, aren't you?' I think they thought I might be swearing and doing Wu-Tang signs. I don't talk to adults like that, why would I talk to children like that? There's a lot of disrespect. I'd give my opinion and a lot of times people would pooh-pooh it. I felt that if the opinion came out of a white person's mouth, the reaction would be different.

The amount of people – super-clever people – I know who have left the field because of a lack of trust or disrespect: it's basic underlying discrimination. I've been lucky enough to get a job where I'm left to do my thing.

You've got to have representation within the workforce and the media. Compared with chemistry and physics, there aren't a lot of POC in biological, natural sciences, ecology and conservation. I can't think of any POC in the BBC Wildlife world when I was starting out. It felt like it was only for a certain type of person.

What else can be done to improve the situation? I'd say asking people of colour for our opinions, listening to our voices. I was sitting at a conference once, listening to someone talk about the subject, getting really annoyed, when there were people of colour who could've been doing that talk.

Return to the source of the wild

As our children grow, we have witnessed their relationship with the animate world develop and deepen and ours, too, in a kind of happy symbiosis. Our hope is that as our children journey through childhood, into adolescence and then adulthood, this will continue, especially at a time when wider relations between humanity and the rest of nature need a reset.

For those who want to fight against the continuing winnowing of nature – and the winnowing of our own and our children's relationship with nature – there is a lot to do. Sometimes it can feel overwhelming. Ken and I find that the best antidote, and a powerful method of restoration and revival, is always to return to the source: simply, to get out and seek the wild, and the surprises and joy and enchantment that may be waiting.

We were in the final crumbs of the year, the strange non-days just before its end. Walks over Christmas had been tricky: the mud was thick, the clouds were dark and heavy, and every time we went out someone fell head-first into a puddle or felt tired or got too cold, and our attempts at spending time in nature were quickly aborted.

On waking, we saw frost twinkling on the house and car roofs on the street, and a dawn sky lightened with coconut-ice pink. If we got out quickly, I figured, there might be ice to play with on a local RSPB heathland that we'd recently discovered. Evie was now four and a half and able to manage longer walks, but the cold, wet weather meant our expectations were kept low. Hot chocolate and (when we remembered them) spare socks and gloves helped, but sometimes a ten-minute scoot about outdoors was all that was manageable. So I wasn't anticipating this walk to be one for the memory books.

Part of the lowland heath was managed by the local council, and the other part by the RSPB as a Site of Special Scientific Interest. It was home to nightjars, tree pipits, woodlarks, Dartford warblers and the silver-studded blue butterfly. Heathland is a good landscape if you're seeking open skies and views. I wanted a visual change from our usual woodlands and the urban street where we live; I wanted to look long-distance and give my eyes a different perspective – a stretch. Lowland heath is, sadly, rare: 75 per cent has been lost in the last 200 years.

We entered from a fast, loud and busy road into a wild and open landscape. Craggy, moss-draped trees formed a woodland to our left, and the heath on the right stretched and glimmered under a light covering of snow, frost and ice. Brambles, thistles, teasels and oak leaves were fringed in sparkling white, and every few metres an iced puddle drew squeals of excitement and wonder from Evie and Max. The ice was more thrilling and engaging than the presents in their Christmas stockings. I was surprised by how much fun they found in it. Jumping on the ice. Stamping on it. Stepping gently on it. Bashing two ice shards together. Throwing it to each other. Cracking it. Snapping it. Looking through it. Letting it melt in their hands. Trying to pick up the biggest piece possible.

'This is a magical ice wonderland!' said Evie again and again, delighting at the new prettiness of a thistle adorned with frost sprinkles and at the crispy rime on plants and leaves. As the sunlight became stronger and less diffuse, which felt welcome on our wintry retinas, patches of moss

Nothing in nature is ever static

became as neon-green as lime jelly. We wandered through an area of silver birch, with red kites flying overhead, looking for fallow deer, enjoying the smell of wood smoke.

The children slid down icy slopes, climbed over frosty grass mounds and made wolf-howl noises to and fro with a couple of older children fifty metres or so away. Max, now eighteen months, pointed out a frosty 'a-caw' (acorn).

'A fairy tree!' The ice and frost had set Evie's imagination spinning and she led us to touch the bark of a magic tree, where we'd receive superpowers from the local fairies. 'This is so beautiful!' she cried, pointing to a bracket fungus that lay like a white cloud suspended in the middle of a tree trunk. I realised that she was now starting to point out as much (or more) to me as I was to her. With red cheeks and ruffled hair, we returned home, feeling revived, contented and awed by the glistening heath and forest, our spirits charged by the wonder and peace of the wild.

Resources

Canal & River Trust
https://canalrivertrust.org.uk

Forestry England
https://www.forestryengland.uk/search-forests

National Nature Reserves (England)
https://www.gov.uk/government/collections/national-nature-reserves-in-england

National Nature Reserves (Northern Ireland)
https://www.daera-ni.gov.uk/topics/land-and-landscapes/nature-reserves

National Nature Reserves (Scotland)
https://www.nature.scot/enjoying-outdoors/scotlands-national-nature-reserves

National Nature Reserves (Wales)
https://naturalresources.wales/guidance-and-advice/environmental-topics/wildlife-and-biodiversity/protected-areas-of-land-and-seas/national-nature-reserves/?lang=en

National Nature Reserves (Ireland)

https://www.npws.ie/nature-reserves

National Trust

https://www.nationaltrust.org.uk

The Rivers Trust

https://www.theriverstrust.org

RHS Gardens

https://www.rhs.org.uk/gardens

RSPB

https://www.rspb.org.uk

Wildfowl & Wetland Trust

https://www.wwt.org.uk

The Wildlife Trusts

https://www.wildlifetrusts.org

Wildlife Watch

https://www.wildlifewatch.org.uk

Woodland Trust

https://www.woodlandtrust.org.uk

EDUCATION-BASED

Council for Learning Outside the Classroom
https://www.lotc.org.uk

EcoActive (East London)
https://ecoactive.org.uk

Eco Schools
https://www.eco-schools.org.uk

Eden Project Schools
https://www.edenproject.com/learn/schools

Jane Goodall's Roots & Shoots
https://www.rootsnshoots.org.uk

Joe Harkness' Bird Therapy Teaching Pack
http://joeharkness.co.uk

Kids Gone Wild
https://kidsgonewild.co.uk

Learning Through Landscapes
https://www.ltl.org.uk/free-resources

Linnean Learning
https://www.linnean.org/learning

London Environmental Educators Forum
www.leef.org.uk

Natural Thinkers (South London)

https://www.naturalthinkers.co.uk

Nature Friendly Schools

https://www.naturefriendlyschools.co.uk

Outdoor Classroom Day

https://outdoorclassroomday.com

Outdoor Play and Learning

https://outdoorplayandlearning.org.uk

Outdoor and Woodland Learning (Scotland)

https://www.owlscotland.org

The Promise

https://www.thepromise.earth/educational-resources

Root and Branch Out (Rutland)

https://www.rootandbranchout.co.uk

Scopes4SEN

https://scopes4sen.weebly.com

Scotland's Finest Woods

http://www.sfwa.co.uk/schools-award

Trees For Learning

https://www.merseyforest.org.uk/our-work/education/
trees-for-learning

Trout in the Classroom / River Chess Association (Bucks)

http://www.riverchessassociation.co.uk/education.html

Under the Trees (Scotland)

https://underthetrees.co.uk

World Ocean Day for Schools

https://worldoceanday.school

WWF Activities

https://www.wwf.org.uk/learn/love-nature/get-making

SPECIES

Bats

www.bats.org.uk

Beaver Trust

https://beavertrust.org

Big Butterfly Count

https://bigbutterflycount.butterfly-conservation.org

The Bug Club / Amateur Entomologists' Society

https://www.amentsoc.org/bug-club

Buglife

https://www.buglife.org.uk

Bumblebee Conservation Trust

https://www.bumblebeeconservation.org

Butterfly Conservation

https://butterfly-conservation.org/butterflies

Caterpillars

https://www.uksafari.com/caterpillars.htm

Froglife

https://www.froglife.org

Marine Conservation Society

https://www.mcsuk.org

Moths

https://ukmoths.org.uk

Plantlife

https://www.plantlife.org.uk/uk

Royal Entomological Society

https://www.royensoc.co.uk

RSPB Big Garden Birdwatch

https://www.rspb.org.uk/get-involved/activities/birdwatch

Whales and dolphins

https://www.orcaweb.org.uk

GENERAL / LOCAL ORGANISATIONS IN THE UK

Action for Conservation
https://www.actionforconservation.org

Ampersand Projects (Birmingham and the Black Country)
http://www.ampersandprojects.org

Backyard Nature
https://www.backyardnature.org

Black2Nature camps
http://www.birdgirluk.com

Birding for All
https://birdingforall.com

Butterflies of Britain (Suffolk and Norfolk)
https://www.butterfliesofbritain.com

Caen Hill Countryside Centre (Devizes)
https://www.caenhillcc.org.uk/about-demo

Cambridge Curiosity and Imagination
https://www.cambridgecandi.org.uk

Country Trust
https://www.countrytrust.org.uk

Cranedale Centre (Malton)
https://cranedale.com

Diversity in Green Spaces (London)
https://www.diversityingreenspaces.org

Dynamic Dunescapes
https://dynamicdunescapes.co.uk

Earth Calling (Edinburgh)
https://www.earthcalling.org

Eco Action Families
https://www.ecoactionfamilies.life

Edinburgh Green Space (Edinburgh)
http://www.elgt.org.uk

Edinburgh Play & Wellbeing
https://edinburghplaywellbeing.co.uk

Fairyland Trust (Norfolk)
http://www.fairylandtrust.org/about

Family John Muir Award
https://www.johnmuirtrust.org/john-muir-award/get-involved/family-support

Farms for City Children
https://farmsforcitychildren.org

Fathers & Nature Dads' Group (London)

https://www.naturevibezzz.org/fathers-nature

Field Study Council

https://www.field-studies-council.org

Fledglings Outdoor Play (East Brighton)

https://m.facebook.com/FledglingsOutdoorPlay/?_rdr

Flock Together (London)

https://www.flocktogether.world/latest/flock-together-is-for-the-children

https://www.instagram.com/flocktogether.world/?hl=en

Friends of the Earth

https://friendsoftheearth.uk

The Garden Classroom (Hackney)

https://www.thegardenclassroom.org.uk

Go Wild With Us (Croydon)

https://www.gowildwithusuk.com

The Green Team (Edinburgh)

https://www.greenteam.org.uk

Grow – Wellbeing

https://www.grow-wellbeing.com

Hogacre Common (Oxford)

http://www.hogacrecommon.org.uk

Imayla (Bristol)
http://www.imayla.com

Incredible Edible Network
https://www.incredibleedible.org.uk

Inspero (Basingstoke, Hants)
https://www.inspero.org.uk

Iver Environment Centre (Bucks)
http://iverenvironmentcentre.org

Land in our Names
https://landinournames.community

Let's Go Outside & Learn (Hounslow)
https://www.lgoal.org

Minstead Study Centre (New Forest)
https://www.friendsofminstead.org.uk

Morecambe Bay Partnership (Kendal)
https://www.morecambebay.org.uk

Moulsecoomb Forest Garden and Wildlife Project (Brighton)
https://moulsecoombforestgarden.org

National Botanic Garden of Wales
https://botanicgarden.wales/science/growing-the-future

National Trust – 50 Things to Do

https://www.nationaltrust.org.uk/50-things-to-do

Nature Days (Gower, Wales)

https://naturedays.co.uk

Nature's Child

https://davidroberts806.lpages.co/natures-child

NYCE (Bristol)

https://www.nyce.org.uk/services

The Orchard Project

https://www.theorchardproject.org.uk

The Outdoors Project (Hove)

https://www.theoutdoorsproject.co.uk

Playing Out

https://playingout.net

Parents for Future

https://www.parentsforfuture.org.uk

Port Sunlight River Park / Autism Together

https://www.autismtogether.co.uk/port-sunlight-river-par

Rainbows / Brownies / Guides

https://www.girlguiding.org.uk/information-for-parents/
register-your-daughter

Roam

http://www.roam.org.uk

Rowanbank (Edinburgh)

https://www.rowanbank.org.uk

Scouts UK

https://www.scouts.org.uk

Secret Seed Society

http://secretseedsociety.com

Small Seeds Theatre Company

https://www.smallseedstheatrecompany.com

Social Farms & Gardens

https://www.farmgarden.org.uk

Sprout Up Garden / Believe in Tomorrow (London)

https://www.sproutup.co.uk/believe-in-tomorrow

Strickley Farm (Kendal)

https://www.visitmyfarm.com

Tadpoles and Twigs (Sussex)

https://www.facebook.com/tadpolesandtwigs

Time to Play (Colchester, Essex)

https://www.timetoplayearlyyears.com

Together We Grow (Essex)
https://www.activeessex.org/together-we-grow-at-home

Trees for Cities
https://www.treesforcities.org

The Urban Birder
http://theurbanbirder.com

We Be Kids
https://www.webekids.net

Wild in the City
https://wildinthecity.org.uk

Wild Tots
https://wildtots.org.uk

Woodcraft Folk
https://dreambigathome.uk

XR Educators
https://www.facebook.com/XRLearningRebellion

LINKS FROM THE BOOK

Allotment information
https://www.gov.uk/apply-allotment

Forager's Association
https://foragers-association.org

Foraging walks
https://www.foragelondon.co.uk

Galloway Wild Foods
https://gallowaywildfoods.com

How to make a seed bomb
https://www.wildlifetrusts.org/actions/how-make-seed-bomb

Humane rat deterrent
https://www.rspca.org.uk/adviceandwelfare/wildlife/deterrents

Microscopy photographer
http://oeggerli.com

Puss moth video
https://www.youtube.com/watch?v=jyAelAH8UFc

RSPB bird names

https://www.rspb.org.uk/birds-and-wildlife/wildlife-guides/
bird-a-z

Woodland Trust's Foraging Guide

https://www.woodlandtrust.org.uk/visiting-woods/things-
to-do/foraging

Tower Hamlets Cemetery Park

www.fothcp.org – London's most urban woodland and
one of the city's 'Magnificent 7' Victorian cemeteries

SPECIALIST KIT / EQUIPMENT

Acrylic paint pens

Bug pots

Fire steel

Hammock

Hand trowel

Magnifying glass

Paracord

Pruning saw

Whittling – the Mora Safe is a fixed safety knife. This means that the edge is razor-sharp, but the point is blunt.

APPS

Big Butterfly Count

Chirp

Forestry England: Forest Xplorer

Go Jauntly

iNaturalist

National Trust: Days Out

Nature Finder (contains more than 2,000 nature reserves)

PictureThis

RSPB: Giving Nature a Home

SkyMap

The Woodland Trust: British Trees

Acknowledgements

Our thanks to our wonderful editor Helen Conford, who conceived the idea with us. Much gratitude to Jessica Woollard, a wise, creative and guiding light. Thank you to the wonderful team at Profile – Cindy Chan, Nathaniel McKenzie, Steve Panton, Lottie Fyfe, Mandy Greenfield, Anna-Marie Fitzgerald, Steve Gove and Chris Bell, James Alexander for the brilliant design, and Mouni Feddag for the joyful, vibrant cover.

Lucy: Thank you to the experts and activists who gave me their time, the pupils at St Mark's Primary School, and especially Donna, for making the visit happen. Thank you to Ken, for being such a pleasure to work and write with, and for teaching me so much. My thanks to my family: Mum and Dad, for taking me out as a child, even when I was ratty about it (!), Ed and Marlene, Brenda and Diarmuid, my children, and, in abundance, to Jim.

Kenneth: There are so many people you meet in life as you move along the road of your chosen profession. As you would expect, there are so many to thank and acknowledge, there just isn't the room here to name-check everyone, so apologies to those that are missed. So, in no particular order here they are. To begin, I'd like to thank my co-author, Lucy Jones – you're an inspirational writer and I couldn't think of anyone better to write my first book with. Thank you for being a brilliant guide to help me navigate my contribution to the book. You made my first experience an extremely pleasurable and enjoyable process. Thank you. Terry Lyle – Tower Hamlets' very own David Attenborough and my mentor and friend since 2002. The Friends of Tower Hamlets Cemetery Park and Tower Hamlets Cemetery Park – the very best place to work. Dimuthu Meehitiya, best friend and superb environmental educator. To all the volunteers I work with, I'd like to think we've taught each other so much, and thank you for giving your most precious commodity of time! Finally, and by no means least, my family: Zoe, Amelia and Elsie – I love that we explore the wilds together and I love you all so much. Thank you all, to those mentioned here by name and those missed. You are all extremely special to me, and thanks for all the guidance, advice, information, freedom and instruction over the years.

Index